The
PRIMARY STEM
IDEAS BOOK

D1388471

The Primary STEM Ideas Book is designed to promote the integrated teaching of STEM in the primary classroom by providing teachers with lesson ideas for investigations and projects. The statutory requirements of the National Curriculum for science, mathematics and design and technology are comprehensively covered through a variety of practical, stimulating and engaging activities, which have all been tried and tested in the primary classroom. The interrelationship between the STEM subjects is strongly integrated throughout, allowing children's knowledge and skills to develop with confidence in these key subjects through activities that only require easily accessible resources generally found in the classroom.

Written by subject specialists with years of classroom experience teaching STEM subjects, each chapter contains:

- A rationale showing links to the National Curriculum
- Key subject knowledge
- Brief activity plans
- Ideas for supporting higher and lower attaining children
- Follow-up ideas to provide extra inspiration

Including 'how to' guides and other photocopiable resources, this book is perfect for creating integrated lessons, group work and discussions relating to STEM. *The Primary STEM Ideas Book* provides easy to follow instructions and helps spark fresh inspiration for both new and experienced teachers in primary STEM education.

Dr Elizabeth Flinn worked in cancer research before retraining to become a primary science specialist. She taught KS2 and KS3 science in a variety of schools in the state and independent sectors for over a decade. She is now a Lecturer in primary science and design and technology education at Middlesex University in London.

Dr Anne Mulligan is a Senior Lecturer at Middlesex University in London where she teaches primary mathematics on the Initial Teacher Education programmes. She has over 20 years of experience teaching in the primary classroom, specialising in KS1, and spent four years as a Deputy Head Teacher before moving to teacher education.

The
PRIMARY STEM IDEAS BOOK

Engaging Classroom Activities Combining Mathematics, Science and D&T

Elizabeth Flinn and Anne Mulligan, with Hannah Thompson

Routledge
Taylor & Francis Group

LONDON AND NEW YORK

First published in 2019
by Routledge
2 Park Square, Milton Park, Abingdon, Oxon, OX14 4RN

and by Routledge
52 Vanderbilt Avenue, New York, NY 10017

Routledge is an imprint of the Taylor & Francis Group, an informa business

British Library Cataloguing-in-Publication Data
A catalogue record for this book is available from the British Library

Library of Congress Cataloging-in-Publication Data
A catalog record has been requested for this book

ISBN: 978-1-138-34053-4 (hbk)
ISBN: 978-1-138-34054-1 (pbk)
ISBN: 978-0-429-44061-8 (ebk)

Typeset in Palatino and Gill Sans
by Newgen Publishing UK

MIX
Paper from
responsible sources
FSC   FSC® C013056
www.fsc.org

Printed and bound in Great Britain by
TJ International Ltd, Padstow, Cornwall

Contents

Acknowledgements   *vii*

1 INTRODUCTION TO STEM   **1**
References   3

2 HOW TO USE THIS BOOK   **4**
Organisation   4
Curriculum links   4
Photocopiable resources   5
STEM or STEAM?   5
Curriculum map   6

3 IT'S ABOUT TIME   **14**
Overview   15
Health and safety   15
Sundials   15
Water clocks   17
Candle clocks   19
Gravity clocks   21
Alarm clocks   23
Tracking the Sun   26

4 PATTERN   **35**
Overview   36
Health and safety   36
Are you *Vitruvian Man*?   36
Fibonacci and the golden rectangle   38
Symmetry in nature   42
Number patterns   45
3-D shape bubbles   49
Cargoes   51

5 A TO B   **57**
Overview   58
Health and safety   58
Egg race   58
Defying gravity (seed dispersal)   61
Post a crisp   63
Animal antics   65
Is fastest best?   68
Cable cars and lifts   70

6 PLANT MAGIC   **76**

Overview   77
Health and safety   77
Pea mazes   77
Living walls   80
Meet a tree   83
Grow a meal   85
Plants for building   88
Sunflower race   90

7 HELP!   **97**

Overview   98
Health and safety   98
Heliographs   98
Buoyancy aids   100
Wind chill   103
Whistles   105
Compasses   107
Beachcombing   109

8 CHOCOLATE   **115**

Overview   116
Health and safety   116
How strong is chocolate?   116
Percentages   118
Chocolate wrappers   120
Flat-pack building   122
Making chocolate   125
Market research   127

9 UP, UP AND AWAY   **133**

Overview   134
Health and safety   134
Paper planes   134
Jet engines   136
Rockets   138
Catapults   140
Parabolas   142
Payloads   144

10 STEM BEYOND THE CURRICULUM   **152**

Overview   153
Health and safety   153
Who forged the cheque?   153
Chain reaction   155
Building with triangles   158
Sorting machines   160
Packing puzzles   162
Makey Makey   165

Acknowledgements

The authors are very grateful to the children and teachers who enthusiastically tested the activities in this book. We thank:

The head teacher, staff and children of Chenies Primary School.
The head teacher, staff and children of Merchant Taylors' Prep.
The head teacher, staff and children of The Annunciation Catholic Infant School.
The staff and children at Ride High in Milton Keynes.

A special mention for: Charlie B., Ethan, Jayesh, Beth, Jocelyn, Michael, Matthew, James F., Emma, Paul, Madeline, Nia, Daisy, Izzie, James D. and Charlie D. who cheerfully helped out in the school holidays and at weekends.

Professor David Sharp and Dr Sally Organ of the School of Engineering and Innovation at the Open University have generously allowed us to adapt some of their ideas for use in the book.

Beth Ellis from Bear Creek Elementary School provided helpful information about the STEM subject curricula in the USA.

NRICH at the University of Cambridge has kindly allowed us to use and adapt some of its activities with Cuisenaire® rods. The authors are using the term Cuisenaire® rods – a trademark registered to Education Solutions (UK) Ltd – with permission.

CHAPTER 1

Introduction to STEM

STEM is widely recognised as the subjects science, technology, engineering and mathematics combined together and taught through an integrated approach. There is growing awareness globally of the importance of STEM education in developing learners as effective problem-solvers who can work constructively as part of a team. The ability to reason mathematically, think critically, solve problems and work collaboratively with others are important skills, sought after by employers today. These are considered by many, including Corlu, Capraro and Capraro (2014), Fitzallen (2015) and Meyrick (2011) to be the key skills of the 21st century.

According to Meyrick (2011), STEM education was first used in the United States as a means of further extending students who were highly talented or who were motivated to deepen their learning. The experience was similar in Australia where STEM opportunities were provided for students who were considered to be gifted in those particular subjects (Fitzallen 2015) and in Turkey where the selection process of schools determined the quality of the STEM education students received (Corlu et al. 2014). Many countries are beginning to see the value of STEM for economic development and are working to improve provision of STEM education in schools. West (2012) believes that countries need to keep up to date with innovation or risk being left behind. He states that 'innovation, particularly through the application of science and technology, is central to maintaining productivity, economic growth, and our standard of living' (West 2012, p. 4). He also makes the point that if a country's capacity for innovation is to be maintained and improved it needs workers who are competent in STEM.

Much of the research on STEM comes from the US and Australia, countries that have carried out research on the benefits of an integrated approach to STEM education on students' learning. Integrating STEM subjects does not mean that all subject disciplines have to be combined. Connections can be made across two or more subjects as long as they are linked 'so that learning becomes connected, focused, meaningful, and relevant to learners' (Smith and Karr-Kidwell 2000, p. 24). Therefore, STEM learning can be seen as interdisciplinary because it involves more than one discipline and the disciplines are interrelated. The curriculum in the primary classroom is particularly suited to this interdisciplinary approach as teachers are expected to teach all subjects and therefore to have good subject knowledge in these subjects. According to Treacy and O'Donoghue (2014), it is important that learners engage in plenty of hands-on group work and have opportunities for enquiry and for discussions throughout. It is also important to introduce STEM activities as early as possible so that learners can develop key skills of problem-solving, critical thinking and mathematical reasoning from an early age. Teaching in this way helps to develop learners' deeper understanding as they experience topics that interest them in real-life contexts (Meyrick 2011). As a result, they are more engaged in their learning and, according to Meyrick (2011), developing these key skills through the teaching of STEM supports pupils from diverse backgrounds so that they have equal opportunities.

There are numerous implications for teachers to consider when teaching integrated STEM activities. The most important of these is their approaches to teaching. More traditional approaches are less effective when it comes to integrating STEM subjects. Teachers need to develop more empowering pedagogies that engage pupils and provide opportunities for enquiry-based learning, creativity and collaborative work (Fitzallen 2015; Meyrick 2011; Stohlmann, Moore and Roehrig 2012). Teachers also need to have a depth of subject knowledge that enables them to feel confident in teaching STEM through an integrated approach. Research by Stohlmann et al. (2012) found that if teachers lacked sufficient subject knowledge in a particular STEM subject then their teaching of STEM would be less effective. Gaps in teachers' subject knowledge or inexperience of teaching a particular subject can lead to teachers doubting their own capabilities. According to Stohlmann et al. (2012, p. 32), 'teachers' content knowledge, experience and pedagogical content knowledge have a large impact on self-efficacy'. Hudson, English, Dawes, King and Baker (2015) noted from their research that 'teaching strategies employed during the STEM lessons facilitated positive attitudes in students to engage with the concepts and the tasks'. The implication for schools that wish to adopt STEM education is that they will need to consider professional development opportunities for teachers so that they receive training in how to develop pedagogic approaches more appropriate for teaching integrated STEM.

Integrated STEM education has implications for curriculum planning as the school curriculum structure may not have the flexibility to allow for this approach to teaching. Teachers may also need support with planning in a more interdisciplinary way, which will differ to discrete subject planning. More time will be needed initially for teachers to plan in this way until they become more familiar and confident with this approach. Resourcing is a further consideration when teaching STEM due to the increase in hands-on practical activities. This may impact on the space available for storage as well as available funding as more resources are needed.

The benefits of STEM education are evident from research by Fitzallen (2015), Meyrick (2011) and Stohlmann et al. (2012), who agree on the positive impact it has on pupils' learning. Meyrick (2011) explains how problem-solving approaches can improve learners' critical thinking skills as well as their understanding of process and their ability to communicate effectively. Stohlmann et al. (2012) discuss how learners can become better problem-solvers who are self-reliant and have a more positive attitude to school. Corlu et al. (2014, p. 75) believe that the 'overarching goal of STEM education is to raise the current generation with innovative mindsets'.

Research carried out in the US by Xie, Fang and Shauman (2015) indicates that although test scores are on a par for boys and girls when comparing mathematics and science, there is a gender gap when it comes to girls continuing STEM to third-level education and beyond. Sax, Kanny, Riggers-Piehl, Whang and Paulson (2015) attribute the lack of engagement of older girls in STEM subjects to their lack of confidence in mathematics rather than their mathematical ability. However, they believe that this may change in the future with more women being attracted into all STEM fields.

This book is designed to promote the teaching of STEM in the primary classroom. The activities are suitable for learners from Year 1 to Year 6 and can be adapted and simplified as necessary for a specific year group. The activities within the chapters can be taught as part of a half-term topic, a STEM week or as individual lessons. The interrelationship and connection between the subjects come across strongly in the activities and in the skills needed to complete them. The activities are all hands-on, as recommended by Treacy and O'Donoghue (2014) and there are obvious opportunities for children to engage in group work and discussion. The chapters contain a number of enquiry questions that children have to investigate through trial and improvement or by adopting a systematic approach. As discussed earlier, it is not necessary to have all the STEM subjects combined for every activity and there are some examples within the chapters where the focus is on two subjects rather than all four. The resources used for each activity are easily accessible and many are everyday objects found in the home. This should make it easier for teachers in terms of cost and storage. The layout of each activity should make planning less time consuming as it contains many pieces of key information that can be copied and pasted onto a lesson plan.

REFERENCES

Corlu, M. S., Capraro, R. M. & Capraro, M. M. (2014) Introducing STEM education: implications for educating our teachers for the age of innovation, in *Education and Science*, 39 (171), pp. 74–85.

Fitzallen, N. (2015) STEM education: what does mathematics have to offer?, in M. Marshman, V. Geiger & A. Bennison (eds). *Mathematics Education in the Margins* (Proceedings of the 38th annual conference of the Mathematics Education Research Group of Australasia), pp. 237–244. Sunshine Coast: MERGA.

Hudson, P., English, L., Dawes, L., King, K. & Baker, S. (2015) Exploring links between pedagogical knowledge practices and student outcomes in STEM education in primary schools, in *Australian Journal of Teacher Education*, 40 (6), pp. 134–151.

Meyrick, K. M. (2011) How STEM education improves student learning, in *Meridian K-12 School Computer Technologies Journal*, 14 (1) https://meridian.ced.ncsu.edu/archive/summer2011/index.html (accessed 28/11/2018).

Sax, L. J., Kanny, M. A., Riggers-Piehl, T. A., Whang, H. & Paulson, L. N. (2015) 'But I'm not good at math': the changing salience of mathematical self-concept in shaping women's and men's STEM aspirations, in *Research in Higher Education: Journal of the Association for Institutional Research*, 56 (4), Springer.

Smith, J. & Karr-Kidwell, P. J. (2000) *The Interdisciplinary Curriculum: A Literary Review and a Manual for Administrators and Teachers* https://files.eric.ed.gov/fulltext/ED443172.pdf (accessed on 1/3/2019).

Stohlmann, M., Moore, T. J. & Roehrig, G. H. (2012) Considerations for teaching integrated STEM education, in *Journal of Pre-College Engineering Education Research (J-PEER)*, 2 (1), Article 4, pp. 28–34.

Treacy, P. & O'Donoghue, J. (2014) Authentic integration: a model for integrating mathematics and science in the classroom, in *International Journal of Mathematical Education in Science and Technology*, 45 (5), pp. 703–718.

West, M. (2012) STEM education and the workplace, in *Occasional Paper Series* Issue 4 www.chiefscientist.gov.au/wp-content/uploads/OPS4-STEMEducationAndTheWorkplace-web.pdf (accessed on 30/11/2018).

Xie, Y., Fang, M. & Shauman, K. (2015) STEM education, in *Annual Review of Sociology*, 41, pp. 331–357 http://doi.org/10.1146/annurev-soc-071312-145659 (accessed on 30/11/2018).

CHAPTER 2

How to use this book

All the activities in this book have been tested by children aged 6 to 11. The authors, illustrator and children have had a great deal of fun designing and testing everything and it is our hope that we have provided enough information and guidance to allow many more children and adults to enjoy and be inspired by the activities. STEM is engaging, challenging and relevant and we think these activities reflect this.

ORGANISATION

This book is organised into themed chapters although each activity can stand alone. All the activities in one chapter could be used for a whole-school STEM event or one or two activities from different chapters could be chosen to support a particular science or mathematics topic.

Each activity has a suggested Introduction and Plenary along with activity notes, but there are always other ways to introduce and summarise the activities.

We have endeavoured to keep resources as simple and cheap as possible. If specialist resources are recommended for an activity then, where possible, an alternative resource is also described. Because the resources are easy to find, the activity ideas can also be used as home-based projects, when children and adults work together to produce a product for a special event or competition at school.

CURRICULUM LINKS

Each activity has links to the Primary National Curriculum for mathematics and science. These links (taken directly from the 2013 Primary National Curriculum document) can be used to support learning in both or either subject. Every activity has the most relevant Primary National Curriculum links highlighted and these are summarised in the Curriculum map at the end of this chapter. There may be other links too, do not feel constrained by our suggestions!

All activities include planning, designing and making skills linked to the design and technology (D&T) curriculum. An opportunity to evaluate designs and products is included in the suggested plenary sections for the activities. If an activity matches a specific D&T technical knowledge theme, then this is indicated in the Curriculum links section and on the Curriculum map.

Activities are usually suitable for either KS1 or lower/upper KS2. Where possible, we have tried to match the mathematics and science curriculum links to the same key stage or year group. Occasionally this has been impossible due to the rather limited curriculum for science at KS1. However, by using the support or extension suggestions, the activities can be simplified for younger children or made more challenging for older children.

PHOTOCOPIABLE RESOURCES

Many activities have associated photocopiable guides designed for use by children. The text of the guides requires good reading skills so each guide has been illustrated carefully, to show each step in the process as clearly as possible. In many guides, Professor Mouse (Figure 2.1) is also present, demonstrating what the children should do.

Figure 2.1 Professor Mouse

STEM OR STEAM?

There is an increasing interest in STEAM: combining the STEM subjects with the arts. For some of the activities in this book there is a clear arts link, but for others it may be more difficult to make a connection. Table 2.1 suggests some ideas for relevant links.

Table 2.1 Suggested STEAM links

Chapter	Suggested STEAM links
3	Timepieces have been present in homes throughout the centuries. Many are beautifully decorated or sculpted. Visit an historic house or museum to see examples of this.
4	The activities in this chapter are clearly linked to art.
5	All activities about transport link closely to geography. For a more artistic link, consider the design of the postage stamps from different countries. These often reflect important events, locations or people of the country.
6	While out in woodland, make some large natural art. Using branches, dead leaves and rocks, the children can create splendid, temporary artworks. Look at the work of Goldsworthy and Long for examples.
7	The children could explore the idea of being a castaway or lost in the wilderness through drama. The 'Whistles' activity, with its focus on pitch and volume has strong links to the music curriculum.
8	Think about how a rather dull, brown substance is made attractive to eat. Discuss the use of colour, shape and texture. Look at the packaging and think about the decoration, arrangement and use of eye-catching logos and pictures.
9	Flight and space travel have inspired many musical compositions. Listen to Holst's *Planets* suite or the atmospheric soundtrack to the film *Apollo 13*.
10	Focus on interesting and exciting architectural designs when building with triangles. Think about the ways architects have solved the problem of holding a roof up and creating an inspiring, beautiful space under it.

CURRICULUM MAP

The year groups for which the activity is most suited, in terms of curriculum requirements, are shown for mathematics and science:

- The mathematics topics are grouped under the Primary National Curriculum headings where they relate specifically to the activities in the chapter. Understanding of number and calculations are not referred to specifically as they are intrinsic to all aspects of mathematics. However, in Chapter 4 some components of number have been highlighted.
- Mathematical reasoning skills are embedded into most of the activities.
- Science topics are grouped under the Primary National Curriculum headings. For simplicity, the various materials topics have been grouped together so that Y1: Everyday materials; Y2: Uses of everyday materials; Y4: States of matter; and Y5: Properties and changes of materials are all included under the 'Materials' heading. The Y1 topic seasonal changes has been included under the heading 'Space'.
- Working scientifically skills such as making observations, taking measurements and recording data are embedded into many of the activities.
- The working scientifically enquiry themes – Fair testing (FT); Observing over time (OT); Identifying and classifying (IC); Pattern seeking (PS); and Researching using secondary sources (R) – are identified where appropriate.
- Occasionally, an activity has no direct link to the mathematics or science curriculum. However, children will have the opportunity to extend their learning in a particular area. This is marked on the Curriculum map with a star (*).
- D&T curriculum requirements have been grouped under six broad headings: Structures; Mechanisms; Food; Textiles; Electronics; and Control. These show the technical subject knowledge covered. Apart from the Electronics and Control sections (KS2 only), the activities meet the requirements for both key stages. All activities require planning, making and evaluation skills.

The Curriculum map has been compiled for the Primary National Curriculum in England but using the Curriculum map in combination with the more detailed links given in each chapter, it should be possible to map the activities to other curricula. All the activities in the book can be linked to International Primary Curriculum topics and many are compatible with the Common Core for Math and Next Generation Science Standards used in the United States.

Table 2.2 Curriculum map for mathematics

	Mathematics							
	Number: fractions	Number: multiplication and division	Ratio and proportion	Algebra	Measurement	Geometry – properties of shapes	Geometry – position and direction	Statistics
Sundials					1, 2, 3		5	
Water clocks		3			1, 3, 4			3
Candle clocks		3			3, 4			3
Gravity clocks					3, 4			3
Alarm clocks					2, 3			
Tracking the sun					2			2
Are you *Vitruvian Man?*	2, 3		6		2, 3			2, 3
Fibonacci and the golden rectangle				6		3, 4		
Symmetry in nature						2, 4		
Number patterns				6				
3-D shape bubbles						2, 3, 6		
Cargoes						2, 4		
Egg race					2, 5			
Defying gravity					2, 4, 5			2, 5
Post a crisp					2			
Animal antics		3			2			2
Is fastest best?					2, 3, 5			2
Cable cars					2			
Pea mazes					1, 2		2	2
Living walls						1, 3		
Meet a tree					1, 2, 4, 5	6		
Grow a meal					2, 3, 5			
Plants for building					2	5		2
Sunflower race					2, 3, 5			2, 4

(continued)

Table 2.2 (Cont.)

	Mathematics							
	Number: fractions	Number: multiplication and division	Ratio and proportion	Algebra	Measurement	Geometry – properties of shapes	Geometry – position and direction	Statistics
Heliographs						5		
Buoyancy aids					5, 6			
Wind chill					2			2, 4, 5
Whistles								4, 5, 6
Compasses							*	
Beach-combing					2			
How strong is chocolate?					3, 4			4
Percentages	5		6		3			
Chocolate wrappers						2, 6		
Flat-pack building						6		
Making chocolate					2, 5			
Market research								2, 3
Paper planes					2, 6			5, 6
Jet engines					2, 3			
Rockets					2			
Catapults					2			
Parabolas					2	5		6

	Mathematics							
	Number: fractions	Number: multiplication and division	Ratio and proportion	Algebra	Measurement	Geometry – properties of shapes	Geometry – position and direction	Statistics
Payloads					2			
Who forged the cheque?								
Chain reaction								
Building with triangles						1, 2, 3, 4, 6		
Sorting machines								
Packing puzzles							2	
Makey Makey								

Table 2.3 Curriculum map for science and D&T

	Science									
	Plants	Living things	Animals inc. humans	Materials	Forces	Space (Seasons)	Sound	Light	Rocks	Electricity
Sundials						5		3, 6		
Water clocks				1, 4						
Candle clocks				5						
Gravity clocks					5					
Alarm clocks										4, 6
Tracking the Sun						1, 5		3, 6		
Are you *Vitruvian Man?*			1, 2, 5							
Fibonacci and the golden rectangle	1, 3	4, 6	1							
Symmetry in nature	1, 3		1							
Number patterns										
3-D shape bubbles		*						3, 6		
Cargoes					*					
Egg race				2, 5	3, 5					
Defying gravity	1, 3				5					
Post a crisp				2, 5	3					
Animal antics			1, 2, 3							
Is fastest best?					3, 5					
Cable cars					5					
Pea mazes	1, 2, 3									
Living walls	1, 2, 3									
Meet a tree	1, 2, 3									
Grow a meal	1, 2, 3		2, 3, 4							
Plants for building				1, 2, 5						
Sunflower race	1, 2, 3									

Evolution	Working scientifically	D&T					
		Structures	Mechanisms	Textiles	Cooking and nutrition	Electronics	Control/IT
	OT						
		•					
	OT						
	PS	•					
						•	
	PS OT						
	PS			•			
	PS						
	PS						
	PS						
		•					
	PS						
		•	•			•	•
6	PS	•					
		•					
	R	•					
	FT		•				
			•				
	OT	•					
		•	•				
	IC						
	R				•		
	FT	•		•			
	OT	•					

Table 2.3 (Cont.)

	Science									
	Plants	Living things	Animals inc. humans	Materials	Forces	Space (Seasons)	Sound	Light	Rocks	Electricity
Heliographs				2				3, 6		
Buoyancy aids					*					
Wind chill				2, 5						
Whistles							4			
Compasses				2	3					
Beach-combing				1, 2			4	3, 6		4, 6
How strong is chocolate?					3					
Percentages				4, 5						
Chocolate wrappers				2, 5						
Flat-pack building				4, 5						
Making chocolate	2		3, 6							
Market research			1							
Paper planes				2	5					
Jet engines					*					
Rockets					*					
Catapults					3, 5					
Parabolas					5					
Payloads					5					
Who forged the cheque?				5						
Chain reaction					5					
Building with triangles				*						
Sorting machines				1, 5	3, 5					
Packing puzzles										
Makey Makey										4, 6

Evolution	Working scientifically	D&T					
		Structures	Mechanisms	Textiles	Cooking and nutrition	Electronics	Control/IT
	PS						
	FT PS						
	OT FT			•			
	PS FT						
		•		•		•	
	FT	•					
	OT PS				•		
		•			•		
		•					
					•		
	*						
	PS FT	•					
			•				
	PS						
	PS						
	FT						
	FT						
	IC						
		•	•			•	
		•					
			•				
	*						
						•	•

CHAPTER 3

It's about time!

3.1 Sundials

3.2 Water clocks

3.3 Candle clocks

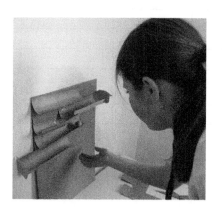

3.4 Gravity clocks

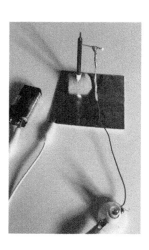

3.5 Alarm clocks

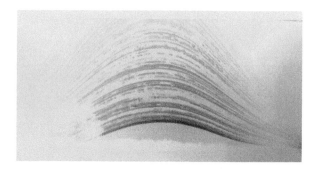

3.6 Tracking the Sun

OVERVIEW

This chapter is all about telling the time, and measuring it. Clocks and timers have been an important part of life for 4000 years and there have been many innovative ways to measure the passing of time. The ability to tell the time or know when something will happen is still important today. Clocks help us to do this now, but how did people manage before the clock as we know it today was invented?

The activities explore some of the earliest and simplest time-measuring devices and show the children how knowing about the properties and behaviour of materials and the Sun can help to produce a functional time measurer.

HEALTH AND SAFETY

Ensure that children never look directly at the Sun.

Candles should be supported securely and surrounded by a non-flammable material such as sand. Make sure long hair is tied back and loose clothing such as ties and scarves are tucked in or removed.

Water and electricity do not mix safely, so if converting water clocks to alarm clocks ensure that the circuits are some distance away from the clocks and protected by being placed in a tray or sandwich box.

Photographic fix should be used in a well-ventilated room and children should wear gloves if they are to come in contact with it.

SUNDIALS

Objective

- To use the apparent movement of the Sun to measure time.

Curriculum links

Mathematics

Y1: **Measurement:** compare, describe and solve practical problems for time (for example, quicker, slower). Measure and begin to record […] time (hours, minutes, seconds). Tell the time to the hour and half past the hour.

Y2: **Measurement:** know the number of minutes in an hour and the number of hours in a day.

Y3: **Measurement:** estimate and read time with increasing accuracy to the nearest minute; record and compare time in terms of seconds, minutes and hours.

Y5: **Geometry:** know angles are measured in degrees: estimate and compare acute, obtuse and reflex angles, draw given angles and measure them in degrees (°).

Science

Y3: **Light:** recognise that shadows are formed when the light from a light source is blocked by an opaque object.

Y5: **Earth and space:** use the idea of the Earth's rotation to explain […] the apparent movement of the Sun across the sky.

Y6: **Light:** use the idea that light travels in straight lines to explain why shadows have the same shape as the objects which cast them.

Background

The Sun has been used to tell the time since prehistoric times. The Sun can be used to measure units of time from seconds to days and months. Sundials are accurate because the Sun's journey across the sky is reliable. However, they don't work at night or on cloudy days. When the Sun's light is blocked, a shadow is formed and as the Sun moves across the sky (it doesn't really move, but it appears to do so because the Earth is spinning) the position of the shadow will also move. Because the Sun follows the same route each day, shadows will be in the same place at the same time each day. During summer, the Sun is higher in the sky so the shadows will all be shorter and in winter, they are much longer.

Activity

Resources

- Stiff card
- Watch or clock
- Pens
- Compass
- Photocopiables: How to make a sundial (p. 29); Gnomons (p. 30).

Introduction

Many children will have already come across sundials so ask who knows about them. Explain, if necessary, about shadow formation and how the shadows move as the Sun's position changes. You might like to demonstrate this with a torch and a book: move the torch around and show the children how the shadow changes position, although it always touches the bottom of the book. Sundials use this movement to show the time. Explain to the children that they are going to make a sundial by marking the position of a shadow as it changes during the day. Show a ready-made sundial and point out the gnomon. Demonstrate how to mark the position of the shadow.

Main session

Children assemble a rudimentary sundial with a gnomon stuck onto the centre of a square of stiff card. Each hour, they should go outside and, placing the sundial in the same position and orientation every time, mark the edge of the gnomon's shadow and label it with the time.

It might help to have a designated 'sundial calibration zone' where there is a template and compass to help the children orientate their sundials correctly.

The next sunny day, the children can test to see whether their sundials are working accurately.

Plenary

Children can feed back about the accuracy of their sundial. Ask about the problems with using a sundial for telling the time. Can they be used over 24 hours? If possible, test the sundials when the clocks change: what happens? It is also interesting to learn what happens if a UK-calibrated sundial is taken abroad. Will it still be useful?

Figure 3.7 Calibrating a sundial at 1 p.m.

Follow-up ideas

Find any local sundials to show the children. They are often in parks, churchyards and stately home gardens.

Make a human sundial. Use a child to be the gnomon and use their shadow to mark off the hours on the playground. To make sure they always stand in the same place, draw round their feet and ensure they always stand in the outline. Draw a long chalk line down the centre of the child's shadow. Other children can be the gnomon at other times, by standing in the same spot. If rain is forecast, then draw the sundial markings onto a large sheet of paper, which can be taken inside if necessary. Have some sort of marking on the paper so that you always put it back down in the correct orientation.

Extension

Mark half and quarter hours and use 24-hour clock labels.

Ask the children to measure the angles between the lines drawn each hour. Are the angles always the same? If so, could they predict where the next hour mark will go?

Support

Pre-assemble the sundial. Ask the children to indicate 'playtime', 'lunchtime' and 'hometime' instead of the clock times.

WATER CLOCKS

Objective

• To use water flowing from a container to measure time intervals.

Curriculum links

Mathematics

Y1: **Measurement:** compare, describe and solve practical problems for: capacity and volume (for example, full/empty, more than, less than, half, half full, quarter), time (for example, quicker, slower), measure and begin to record [...] capacity and volume, time (hours, minutes, seconds), tell the time to the hour and half past the hour.

Y3: **Measurement:** know the number of seconds in a minute, compare durations of events (for example, to calculate the time taken by particular events or tasks).

Y3: **Number: multiplication and division:** solve problems [...] involving multiplication and division, including positive integer scaling problems (for example, 5 times as fast).

Y4: **Measurement:** solve problems involving converting between minutes to seconds.

Science

Y1: **Everyday materials:** describe the simple physical properties of a variety of everyday materials (including water).

Y4: **States of matter:** compare and group materials together according to whether they are solids, liquids or gases. (Non-statutory guidance: pupils should explore a variety of everyday materials and develop simple descriptions of the states of matter.)

Background

The earliest water clocks may have been made about 4000 years ago. The ancient Greeks used a water clock or *clepsydra* that worked by allowing water to flow out of a hole in the bottom of a jar. This was used to measure a fixed amount of time. Ancient Indians used an empty bowl with a hole in the bottom, which sank slowly in a larger bowl of water. Ancient Egyptians also had their own design of water clock. This was a conical bowl with a scale marked in the inside. Water dripped slowly from a small hole in the bottom of the bowl.

Water drips from holes because it is a liquid and can flow. Gravity ensures that drips fall downwards but the rate of dripping is also linked to the volume of water and, hence, water pressure, in the container. This means that full containers often produce faster drips than nearly empty containers.

This is a very wet activity and can be frustrating as water clocks are not very accurate due to the decrease in water pressure as the cup empties. This is a good activity to do outside on a warm day.

Similar clocks can be made using sand. The principle is similar, but the holes in the cup will need to be larger.

Activity

Resources

- Plastic cups or yoghurt pots
- Drawing pins or nails
- Timers
- Waterproof pens
- Jug of water
- Large container or tray to catch spills

Introduction

Show the children water dripping from one leaky cup and filling up another cup and explain that they will use water to make a one-minute timer. They can either use the emptying of a cup or the filling of a second container as a measure of the time interval.

Main session

After making one or several pin holes in the plastic cup, the children can fill it with water and time how long it takes for the water to drip out. They can then adjust the amount of water added to the cup so that they can time a particular period. They should hold the cups as still as possible and collect the drips in a second container. They can mark a fill level on their cup or add a measured volume of water and record the time taken for the water to drip out.

The children may decide to fill a cup and then wait until the water has reached a particular level in the collection container.

Plenary

Check the children's water clocks against an accurate timer. Discuss why the water clocks are not very reliable. Have the children noticed that the full cups drip faster than the nearly empty cups? Have they taken this into account?

Discuss the problems with relying on a water clock to tell the time. How big would it need to be to measure an hour? What would happen if you forgot to refill the container?

Figure 3.8 A water clock in action

Follow-up ideas

There are various other ways to make water clocks and the internet provides some good ideas. The children could try out different ways and decide which clocks are the most accurate ones.

Children could measure the volume of water required to time one minute and then try doubling and tripling the volume to see how the time period changes.

Go large! Use the 5-litre mineral water containers that some supermarkets sell and make a large water clock. You may have to find a suitable stand to hold the container, which will be heavy when filled with water. Remember to have an equally large container in which to collect the drips. The 5-litre water clock in Figure 3.9 has a 1 mm hole in the lid and can time 25 minutes. It is strapped securely to a garden chair. The water is directed from the top bottle to the other down a straw; this makes it easier to catch the drips.

Figure 3.9
A 5 l water clock

Extension

Children could investigate whether different sized cups affect the rate that the same volume of water drips out. If appropriate, you can introduce the idea of water pressure.

Can the children use the same apparatus to make a clock that would measure five minutes? They may have to refill the cup partway through.

Support

Use a sand timer instead of a stop watch if children have difficulty understanding seconds and minutes.

Provide a set of pre-punched plastic cups; some with more holes than others, so the children can investigate how fast the water drips from each cup.

CANDLE CLOCKS

Objective

- To use the irreversible change of burning wax to create a clock.

Curriculum links

Mathematics

> **Y3: Measurement:** know the number of seconds in a minute, compare durations of events (for example, to calculate the time taken by particular events or tasks), measure, compare, add and subtract lengths (m/cm/mm).
> **Y3: Number: multiplication and division:** solve problems […] involving multiplication and division, including positive integer scaling problems (for example, 5 times as fast).
> **Y3: Statistics:** interpret and present data using […] tables.
> **Y4: Measurement:** solve problems involving converting between minutes to seconds.

Science

> **Y5: Properties and changes of materials:** explain that some changes result in the formation of new materials and that this kind of change is not usually reversible, including changes associated with burning […].

Background

Burning is an irreversible change so that once something has burnt it has been changed permanently into something else. Burning candle wax produces CO_2 and carbon (soot) and some water vapour, all of which are lost to the surroundings so that a candle gradually decreases in length as it burns. To burn at a constant rate, candles should be shielded from draughts. Candle clocks were used in ancient China and Japan (from about AD 520). Alfred the Great is also known to have used a candle clock.

Activity

Resources

- Candles (non-drip)
- Candlesticks or jars of sand to stand candles in
- Matches
- Timers measuring minutes and hours
- Ruler
- Pins with large heads

Table 3.1 Candle clock data

Type of candle	5 mins	10 mins
Birthday cake (0.5 cm diameter)	1.5 cm	3 cm
Table candle (1.5 cm diameter)	0.5 cm	1 cm
	10 mins	**1 hour**
Table candle (2.5 cm diameter)	0.5 cm	3 cm

Introduction

Show the children how a small birthday cake candle gets shorter with time and ask them to think about how this might be used as a timer. Discuss what is meant by an irreversible change and discuss what the candle wax might turn in to. Many children struggle to understand that the wax actually disappears, many think it just melts and drips down the candle. Using non-drip candles can help to right this misconception.

Main session

Children measure the length of their candle and record it. They light the candle and allow it to burn for five or ten minutes – this depends on the size of the candle (see Table 3.1). They extinguish the candle and measure it again. The children can calculate the length of candle lost over the time interval. Using a ruler, they measure the same distance on the candle and mark it by carefully pushing a pin into the wax at the correct point or drawing a biro line (Figures 3.10 and 3.11). The candle can then be lit and timed again. At the correct time, all things being well, the candle will have decreased in length to reach the pin, which should fall out.

If lighting a number of candles safely in the classroom is a problem, use the candle-clock data and ask the children to calculate where to mark the candle to show a particular time interval. Then only light the candles at the end of the session in order to see who was most accurate.

Plenary

Children can test their candle clocks by marking the appropriate length and comparing their candle clock to a timer or digital clock. How accurate are the candles?

If children have used different sized candles then they can compare the lengths they measured for the same time interval. If the children have all used identical candles then they should compare their measurements – how accurate has everyone been?

Discuss how accurate the clocks are. Do they work best for measuring seconds or minutes or tens of minutes?

Ask how these candles could act as clocks, to tell the time, rather than just as timers to measure a time interval. What would the user have to know when they lit the candle? How could they use this information and the candle to tell the time later in the day?

Figure 3.10 A five-minute candle clock

Follow-up ideas

Use the measured lengths to predict how much candle will have burnt in different lengths of time then test the predictions.

Al-Jazari, a prolific inventor from the 13th century, made some very sophisticated candle clocks including one that had a dial to show the time. Al-Jazari invented many clocks, some with automata (moving figures) and is well worth reading about.

Extension

The children can work out how far the candle would burn in a different length of time and test their ideas. This needs an understanding of scaling.

Children could investigate different sized candles and see how the time taken to burn a particular distance is linked to the diameter of the candle.

Figure 3.11 A ten-minute candle clock

Support

Thinner candles will burn further in a given time, so that lengths are easier to measure for short time intervals.

Use a sand timer instead of a stopwatch to measure time. The children can measure how far the candle has burned when the sand runs out.

GRAVITY CLOCKS

Objective

* To use falling objects to create a timer.

Curriculum links

Mathematics

Y3: Measurement: know the number of seconds in a minute, compare durations of events (for example, to calculate the time taken by particular events or tasks).
Y4: Measurement: solve problems involving converting between minutes to seconds.
Y3: Statistics: interpret and present data using […] tables.

Science

Y5: Forces: explain that unsupported objects fall towards the Earth because of the force of gravity.

Background

Gravity is an invisible force that pulls all things towards the centre of the Earth. Everything is moved at the same speed and, on Earth, acceleration due to gravity has a constant value of 9.8 m/s^2. This means that if something takes 1 second to fall from a particular height to the ground then, keeping the conditions the same, we can be sure that it will always take exactly the same time to drop. Balls roll down ramps and children slide down slides because gravity is pulling them down. The slope of the ramp or slide will affect the speed the ball or child descends. The shallower the slope of the ramp, the slower the balls will fall.

Activity

Resources

- Firm board such as a small whiteboard, clipboard, chopping board or large table mat
- Card, cardboard tubes and straws to make ramps
- Timer
- Tape
- Scissors
- Marbles, beads or ball bearings
- Marble-run game (if possible)
- Photocopiable: Gravity clock template (p. 31)

Introduction

Explain to the children that they are going to design and make a marble-run-style timer. They should try to get the ball to roll as slowly as possible; ask how they might manage this. If you have a marble-run game, show them how a marble rolls slowly down the shallow runs, compared to the speed that it drops straight down. Discuss how this idea might be used to make a timer.

Main session

The children should tape tubes, and other types of ramp, to the base board. They can test how long it takes their marble to run down the ramps. They will need to adjust the ramps to make them as flat as possible if they want to slow the marble down effectively, so they can use trial and improvement to adjust ramps to the optimum slope. The children may have to add end stops to prevent the balls rolling the wrong way out of the tubes as they drop from one level to the next. Children could also investigate whether different surfaces can help to slow down the ball. They can record their observations in a table and compare the results.

Plenary

The children test their timers; saying first how long they expect it to take the marble to reach the bottom.

Look at the most successful timers to see how the children have solved the problem of 'beating gravity'.

Figure 3.12 A ten-second gravity clock

Follow-up ideas

Gravity clocks like these do exist, but generally only as gimmicks. There is one in the Museum of Discovery and Science in Fort Lauderdale in Florida (the Great Gravity Clock: https://mods.org/exhibits/great-gravity-clock/ and some films on YouTube). Children could discuss why they are not very practical ideas for household clocks.

Figure 3.13 A giant gravity clock under construction

Pendulum clocks use gravity in a different way. Children could investigate more about pendulums and long-case (grandfather) clocks and how they use gravity.

Go large! Using the tubes that carpets and fabrics are rolled around, make a huge gravity clock in the playground or hall. The cardboard tubes can be sliced in half using a saw or knife (the ones in Figure 3.13 were cut using a bread knife). The tubes are fairly light and easy to fasten to a fence or climbing frame using wire plant ties. Use ping-pong balls or tennis balls.

Extension

Ask the children to use different sized balls or balls of different weights. Does the time taken to roll down change if they change the ball?

Can the children design a timer that will show how long a minute is, using the same equipment? In order to do this, they will probably have to release several balls, one after the other and time from the release of the first until the finish of the last (the timer in Figure 3.12 will time a minute if six balls are used; each one being released as soon as the previous one reaches the bottom).

Support

Use a sand timer instead of a stopwatch to measure the time interval required.

Stick the Gravity clock template sheet (see Resources) to the backboard; the children can use the lines as a starting point for their ramps and adjust as required.

Use a marble-run toy and ask the children to build their timer using that instead. It will be larger and sturdier than the cardboard models and this will offer some useful discussion points during the plenary.

ALARM CLOCKS

Objective

* To make a switch to operate a buzzer or bulb in a circuit.

Curriculum links

Mathematics

Y2: **Measurement:** tell and write the time to five minutes, including quarter past/to the hour, know the number of minutes in an hour and the number of hours in a day.

Y3: **Measurement:** estimate and read time with increasing accuracy to the nearest minute.

Science

Y4: **Electricity:** construct a simple series electrical circuit.
Y4: **Electricity:** recognise that a switch opens and closes a circuit and associate this with whether or not a lamp lights.
Y6: **Electricity:** compare and give reasons for variations in how components function including [...] the on/off position of switches.
Y6: **Electricity:** use recognised symbols when representing a simple circuit in a diagram.

D&T

Technical knowledge

KS2: understand and use electrical systems in their products.

Background

Alarms clocks give an audible or visual signal when a particular time is reached. They can be set to go off at a particular time such as half past six, or after a particular time interval such as 25 minutes. Using the clocks described in this chapter, it is possible to convert them to alarm clocks using a simple series circuit and an on/off switch. The switch must be designed to be turned on without human intervention and may require a little innovative thinking!

Activity

Resources

- Circuit components: cells, wire or connectors, bulbs or buzzers
- Conducting materials: paperclips, foil, pins etc.
- Insulating materials: card, plastic, wood etc.
- Scissors, glue, tape, staplers
- Light-dependent resistor (for sundials only)
- Clock: water clock, gravity clock, candle clock or sundial
- Pre-assembled alarm circuit: battery, bulb/buzzer and gap for a switch
- Photocopiable: Alarm clock hint sheet (p. 32)

Introduction

Ask children why we have alarm clocks. Ask them when and for what they might need to set an alarm.

Explain the challenge: to convert their water/sand/candle/gravity clock or sundial into an alarm clock so that, after a particular period of time or at a particular time, it will sound a buzzer or switch on a bulb.

Show the children an alarm circuit and explain that they will need to make a switch that is controlled by the clock to activate the alarm circuit. Recap the structure of a switch: where are the conductors and where are the insulators? What are the roles of each?

Main session

Children design their own clock-activated switches, using appropriate materials. They could use the hint sheet if they require help.

If possible, the children make and test their switches and then set up their clock to work as an alarm clock.

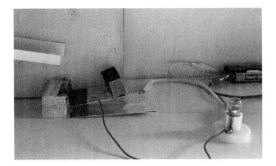

Figure 3.14 A gravity alarm clock

Figure 3.15 A water alarm clock

Plenary

Children describe how their switch will work, focusing on where the conductors are and the mechanics of turning the switch on. If they have made the switch, they can demonstrate it and show how their clock now works as an alarm clock.

Discuss the problems the children came across and solutions they used to solve them.

Follow-up ideas

Find an old clockwork alarm clock and take it to pieces so that the children can see how the alarm is activated.

Challenge the children to convert a clock with hands, such as a classroom clock, to an alarm clock by wiring the circuit so that when the hands reach a particular point on the clock face, the circuit is closed.

Extension

Using a sundial, introduce the children to a light-dependent resistor (LDR). Explain that when there is little or no light shining on the LDR, the resistance in the circuit is high, so that the current will not flow. When there is lots of light shining on the LDR, resistance is reduced and current flows in the circuit. Ask them to think about how to use the LDR as a switch that can be controlled by a sundial.

Ask the children to draw a circuit diagram for their alarm clock.

Support

Use the hint sheet (see Resources) to help children to make a suitable and functioning switch for their clock. The gravity and candle clocks work with very simple switches.

TRACKING THE SUN

Objective

- To observe the Sun's apparent movement across the sky; to describe how day length varies.

Curriculum links

Mathematics

> **Y2: Measurement:** tell and write the time to five minutes, including quarter past/to the hour, know the number of minutes in an hour and the number of hours in a day.
> **Y2: Statistics:** Interpret and construct […] simple tables, ask and answer questions about totalling and comparing categorical data.

Science

> **Y1: Seasonal changes:** Observe and describe […] how day length varies.
> **Y3: Light:** recognise that shadows are formed when the light from a light source is blocked by an opaque object.
> **Y3: Light:** find patterns in the way shadows change.
> **Y5: Earth and space:** use the idea of the Earth's rotation to explain day and night and the apparent movement of the Sun across the sky.
> **Y6: Light:** recognise that light appears to travel in straight lines.

Background

The Earth spins on its axis and, as a result, the Sun appears to travel across the sky each day. The Earth is tilted on its axis and, unless you are on the Equator, this tilt leads to a change in the length of the day during the year. As the Earth tilts towards the Sun, days get longer and the Sun is higher in the sky at midday and when it tilts away, days are shorter and the Sun is much lower at midday. While this can be demonstrated with a globe and a torch, this activity shows how the children can experience the movement of the Sun by tracking its progress across the sky for a day, a month or even six months.

Resources

- Pinhole cameras (cans, tape, card and a pin)
- Black and white photographic paper for example: Ilford Multigrade IV RC glossy paper
- Photographic fix solution also available from Ilford
- Photocopiables: How to make a pinhole camera (p. 33); How to make a clinometer (p. 34)

Introduction

Discuss how the Sun appears to move across the sky each day. The children may know that it shines in though different windows in the morning and afternoon. You may have to help them to observe this.

Show them the pinhole camera and explain how it can 'take a photograph' of the Sun as it moves. The light from the Sun will make a mark on the photo paper. As the Sun moves, so will the mark (Figure 3.16).

Main session

Set up the pinhole cameras. The photo paper is light sensitive, but can be loaded into the pinhole cameras in a dim room without a problem; there is no need for blackout. The children can assemble the cameras and decide where to put them. Using a compass, they should ensure that the pinhole faces south. Leave the cameras for varying amounts of time. Times from one day to six months will give useful information. Once the cameras have been opened, the photos should be fixed by immersing in fix solution for about five minutes and then washing thoroughly in water. Follow manufacturer's instructions for making up the fix solution.

Figure 3.16 A pinhole camera and the six-month photo it took

At the same time, you could start a Sun calendar, which can be used to tell the month. At the same time on the same date each month, mark the length of the shadow of an object. As the Sun gets higher in the sky, the shadow will get shorter. Label each marker with the month and keep going all year. It is helpful if the object producing the shadow is a permanent fixture such as a fence post, and that the marks you make are also permanent. Measure the length of the shadow each month and record in a table. Children can discuss what they notice and if there are any patterns. They could use this to predict the length of the shadow for the next month.

Figure 3.17 A Sun calendar showing that it is October

Plenary

Discuss what the pinhole camera pictures show about the Sun's movement. There will be gaps in the daily track of the Sun and there may be big gaps where no track can be seen for several days. Discuss the reasons for the gaps with the children. It may be helpful to record the weather at the same time as you are recording the Sun's track.

Point out how the track is longer in the summer and shorter in the winter and link this to day length. Discuss how the height of the Sun changes through the year and link this to the length of the shadow on the Sun calendar.

Follow-up ideas

Pinhole-camera photography is an absorbing and interesting hobby. Children may be inspired to try to take photos of buildings and people, rather than the Sun. You can use the same equipment but must work out a correct exposure time and the paper should be developed before it is fixed.

Test the Sun calendar during the next year.

Extension

Children could make and use a clinometer (see Resources) to record the angle of the Sun at midday each week. They should not look through the clinometer but instead stick a piece of card at the end of the viewing tube and tip the clinometer until a circular, black-outlined light spot is projected onto the card (Figure 3.18). The angle will increase and decrease as the seasons change.

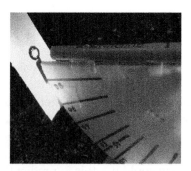

Figure 3.18 Clinometer pointing directly at the Sun

Support

Choose a sunny day to put up the camera and take the paper out the next day or even at the end of the same day so that the children understand that they are seeing the Sun's track for 'now'.

Follow the movement of a shadow at the same time.

How to make a sundial

You will need: [thick card for base] scissors [scissors] marker pen [pen]
thick card for base
thinner card for gnomon compass [compass]
glue [glue] clock [clock]

1. Cut a gnomon and a base board.

   thinner card for gnomon → [] thicker card for base → []   gnomon → [mouse with gnomon and base board] base board

2. Glue the gnomon in the middle of the base board as shown, with space in front, vertical edge of the gnomon forward.

   vertical edge

3. Draw an arrow pointing forwards from the vertical edge of the gnomon.

   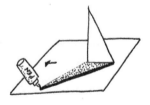
   FRONT

4. Use a compass to find north and line up your sundial's arrow to point north.

5. Mark the edge of the shadow cast by the gnomon, using its sloping edge as your guide.

6. Note the time and mark it on the line.

   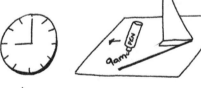
   9am

7. Repeat steps 4-6 every hour.

Figure 3.19

Gnomons

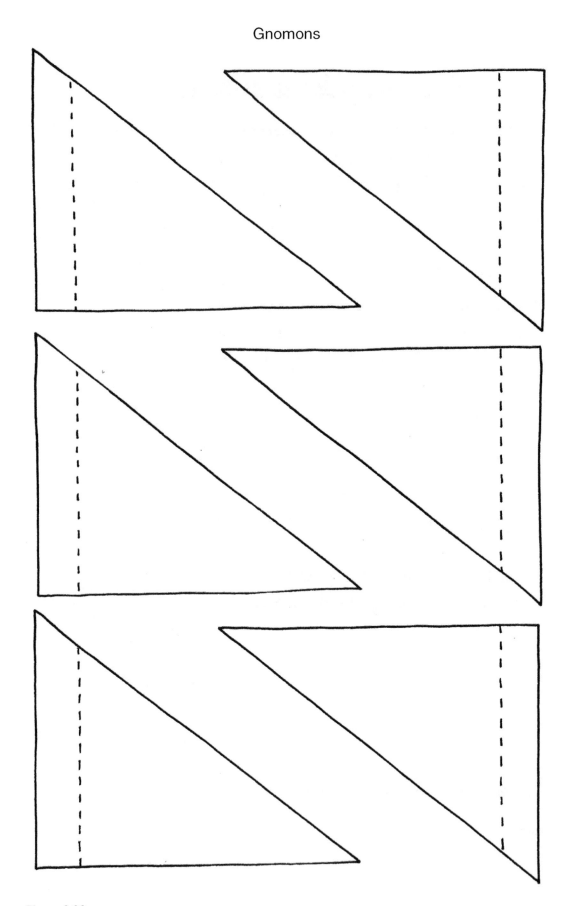

Figure 3.20

Top

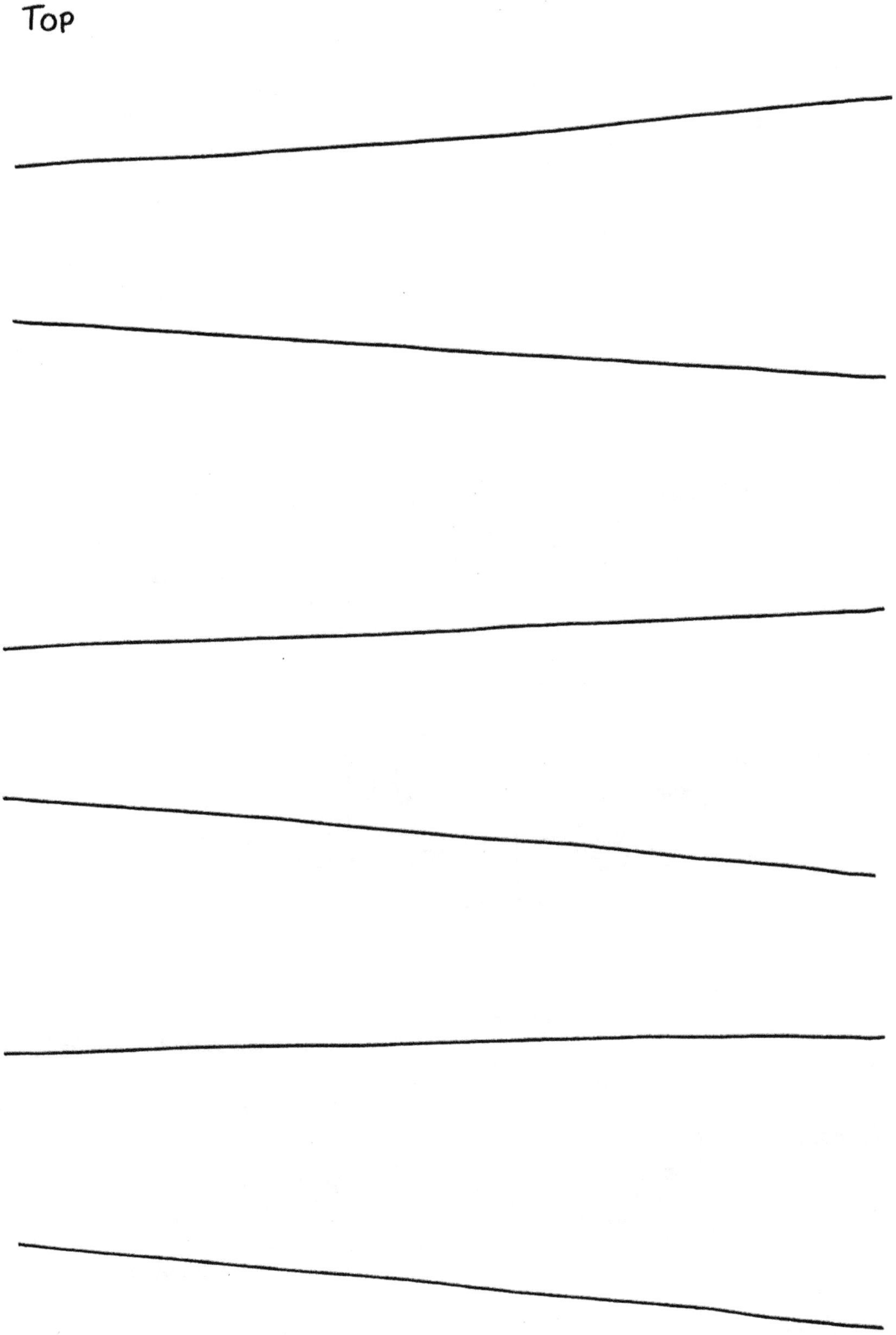

Figure 3.21

Alarm clock hint sheet

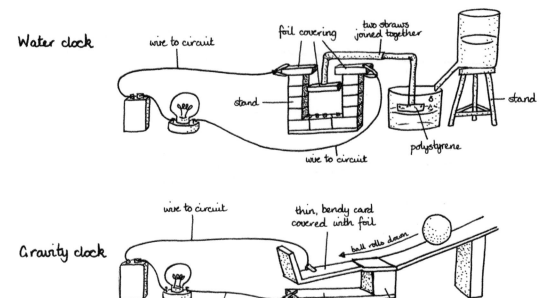

Water clock

wire to circuit — foil covering — two straws joined together — stand — wire to circuit — stand — polystyrene

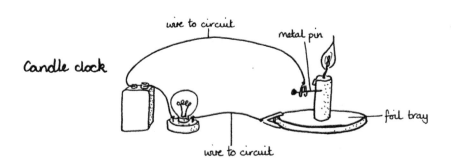

Gravity clock

wire to circuit — thin, bendy card covered with foil — ball rolls down — wire to circuit — card covered with foil — wood block

Candle clock

wire to circuit — metal pin — foil tray — wire to circuit

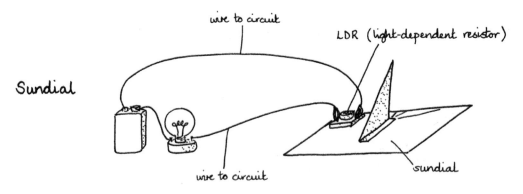

Sundial

wire to circuit — LDR (light-dependent resistor) — wire to circuit — sundial

Figure 3.22

How to make a pinhole camera

You will need:

can with top cut off
or thick cardboard tube
with one end covered

strong waterproof tape
black card
photo paper ☐
masking tape

a pin
scissors ✂
compass ✳
glue

1. Make a close-fitting lid for the can using black card.

 + →  →

2. Cover the can with strong, waterproof tape and, separately, also cover the lid.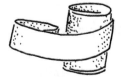

3. Using the pin, make a hole approximately 10cm up the side of the can.

   10 cm

4. Cover the pinhole with a piece of masking tape.

5. In a dark or dim room, insert a sheet of photo paper into the can so that the centre of the paper is opposite the pinhole and the paper curves round the inside wall of the can.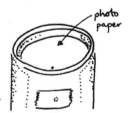

   photo paper

6. Still in the dark room, tape the lid on securely. Avoid covering the masking tape.

7. Site the camera with the pinhole facing south. Once in place, remove the masking tape. You can decide how long to leave the camera in place.

Figure 3.23

How to make a clinometer

You will need:

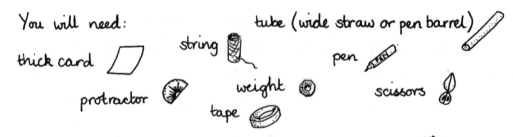

thick card   string   tube (wide straw or pen barrel)   pen

protractor   weight   scissors

tape

1. Cut a quarter circle from the card.

2. Make a notch in one of the straight edges, 1 cm in from the right-angled corner.

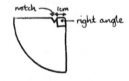

3. Draw a straight line from the notch to the curved edge, parallel to the other straight edge. This is your 0° line.

4. Using a protractor, mark angles from 0° to 90° around the point of the notch.

5. Tape the tube to the notched edge.

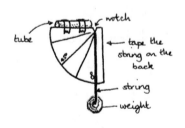

6. Hang the string over the notch, with most hanging down the front. Tape the string to the back of the clinometer. Tie a weight to the string.

7. Look through the tube. The weight will swing as you tilt the clinometer.

Figure 3.24

CHAPTER 4

Pattern

4.1 Are you *Vitruvian Man?*

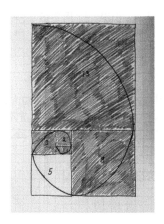

4.2 Fibonacci and the golden rectangle

4.3 Symmetry in nature

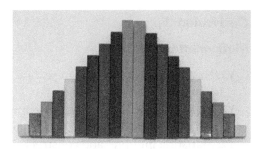

4.4 Number patterns

4.5 3-D shape bubbles

4.6 Cargoes

OVERVIEW

We live in a world full of pattern. We experience it in the clothes we wear, the plants and animals we see and the tasks we do. It is part of our everyday lives. Pattern involves repetition, structure and relationships. Spotting patterns involves identifying these repetitions and structures and the relationships that exist between the different elements. When we recognise a pattern, we can use our reasoning skills to predict the next element in the sequence and make a general statement as to how the pattern will continue.

This chapter focuses on some of the patterns found in the worlds of mathematics and science. The activities show the close relationship between mathematics and science and the importance of pattern in both subjects. Children have the opportunity to explore pattern in the natural world through their engagement with the Fibonacci activity and to investigate mathematical patterns through the use of practical resources.

HEALTH AND SAFETY

Remind the children about safety when using or carrying scissors. Care should be taken when using pins to pierce the paper to avoid pricking fingers.

Make sure the items used as cargo are not a choking hazard.

ARE YOU *VITRUVIAN MAN?*

Objective

- To investigate the proportions of the human body.

Curriculum links

Mathematics

Y2: **Number: Fractions**: recognise, find, name and write fractions $\frac{1}{3}$, $\frac{1}{4}$, $\frac{2}{4}$ and $\frac{3}{4}$ of a length […].

Y2: **Measurement:** choose and use appropriate standard units to estimate and measure length/height in any direction (m/cm) […] to the nearest appropriate unit, using rulers.

Y2: **Statistics:** interpret and construct simple tables.

Y3: **Number: Fractions:** count up and down in tenths; recognise that tenths arise from dividing an object into 10 equal parts and in dividing one-digit numbers or quantities by 10; recognise, find and write fractions of a discrete set of objects.

Y3: **Measurement:** measure, compare, add and subtract: lengths (m/cm/mm).

Y3: **Statistics:** interpret and present data using […] tables.

Y6: **Ratio and proportion:** solve problems involving the relative sizes of two quantities.

Science

Y1: **Animals including humans:** identify, name, draw and label the basic parts of the human body […].

Y2: **Animals including humans:** notice that animals, including humans, have offspring which grow into adults.

Y5: **Animals including humans:** describe the changes as humans develop to old age.

Background

Marcus Vitruvius was a Roman architect who lived during the first century BC. He believed that strength, functionality and beauty were central to any good architectural design. He saw the human body as naturally perfect in terms of proportions and symmetry and believed there was a link between the perfect human body and the laws of nature. In 1490 Leonardo da Vinci sketched the drawing that became known as the *Vitruvian Man*. It depicts a man standing within a circle and a square with arms and legs outstretched. Da Vinci's world-famous image demonstrates the link that is believed to exist between geometry and the proportions of the perfect human form.

This activity could be part of a wider historical topic about famous people or a stand-alone activity related to measurement.

Activity

Resources

- Image of the *Vitruvian Man* by Leonardo da Vinci (images are freely available on-line)
- A range of tape measures, rulers, metre sticks
- Pencils
- Paper

Introduction

Show children an image of the *Vitruvian Man* and discuss Leonardo da Vinci's purpose in drawing the image and his theories about the proportions of the human body. Discuss the different measures involved and how children could test these.

Revise measurements and the importance of measuring accurately. Discuss the different ways of measuring i.e. metre stick, 30 cm ruler, tape measure, marking on a wall/floor and measuring the marks etc.

Main session

Children can decide the best way of testing the hypotheses and how to be systematic with their measurements and record results. Children should work in threes to measure each other and record the results of the following measurements in a table:

- The length of my arm span is equal to my height.
- From my hairline to the bottom of my chin is one-tenth of my height.
- From my elbow to the tips of my fingers is one-quarter of my height.
- The length of my hand is one-tenth of my height.
- My foot is one-seventh of my height.

Figure 4.7 Measuring the width of arm span

Plenary

Compare measurements against the *Vitruvian Man*. What do they notice? How close were their measurements? Why might there be differences?

Follow-up ideas

The measurements could be used to design garments, for example making clothing in D&T. Children could also work out the proportions of a garment to fit themselves based on their own body measurements.

Extension

More detailed measurements could be taken for example:

- The maximum width of my shoulders is one-quarter of my height.
- From below my foot to below my knee is one-quarter of my height.
- The distance from my elbow to my armpit is one-eighth of my height.

Older children could carry out research into the golden ratio and the connection to the proportions of the human body.

Support

Give children a prepared table with fewer body parts to measure. Children could draw around each other on large paper on the floor to make measuring easier or mark height and arm span on paper and measure those. Some younger children may be supported by an adult in order to measure accurately and to read the measurements.

FIBONACCI AND THE GOLDEN RECTANGLE

Objective

- To recognise and understand the Fibonacci sequence and use it to draw the golden rectangle and golden spiral.

Curriculum links

Mathematics

Y3: Geometry: draw 2-D shapes, recognise angles as a property of shape or a description of a turn.

Y4: Geometry: compare and classify geometric shapes, including quadrilaterals and triangles, based on their properties and sizes.

Y5: Number: number and place value: (non-statutory guidance) recognise and describe linear number sequences […] and find the term-to-term rule.

Y6: Algebra: use simple formulae, generate and describe linear number sequences.

Science

Y1: Plants: identify and describe the basic structure of a variety of flowering plants, including trees.

Y1: Animals including humans: describe and compare the structure of a variety of common animals.

Y3: Plants: explore the part that flowers play in the life cycle of flowering plants, including pollination, seed formation and seed dispersal.

Y4: Living things and their habitats: recognise that living things can be grouped in a variety of ways.

Y6: Living things and their habitats: describe how living things are classified into broad groups according to common observable characteristics and based on similarities and differences, including micro-organisms, plants and animals.

Background

Leonardo of Pisa was an Italian mathematician who was born in 1170. He was known as Fibonacci (son of Bonacci) and gave his name to the Fibonacci sequence of numbers. This sequence is a series of numbers (0, 1, 1, 2, 3, 5, 8 ...) where each term is found by adding the two preceding numbers in the sequence. Fibonacci noticed this pattern when he was attempting to solve a problem involving breeding rabbits.

Activity

Resources

- Pencils
- Paper
- Squared paper
- Colouring pencils
- Calculators
- Rulers (optional)

Introduction

Introduce the number sequence 0, 1, 1, 2, 3, 5, 8 ... and let the children explore and discuss what they notice about the numbers. They can draw the sequence on squared paper or use Cuisenaire® rods to show a visual representation of the sequence. Can children work out the next number in the sequence and explain their reasoning?

Figure 4.8 Exploring the Fibonacci sequence with Cuisenaire rods

Main session

Introduce the children to the Fibonacci sequence and how it is constructed. Explain its relevance in geometry and its connection to the golden ratio. The golden ratio is found by dividing one of the Fibonacci numbers by a preceding number, e.g. 8 divided by 5. Children can test this for themselves using a calculator and working their way through the sequence of numbers. What do they notice about their answers as they work with larger numbers?

We can use Fibonacci's numbers to create the golden rectangle. Using squared paper draw a square of length 1. Draw another square of length 1 adjoining and to the right of the original square.

Draw a square of length 2 above the other two squares and a square of length 3 to the left of the original squares (Figure 4.9).

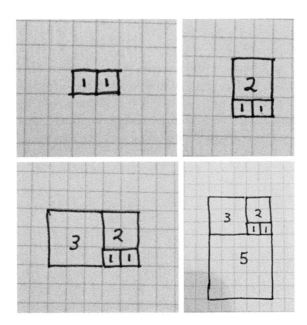

Figure 4.9 Drawing a golden rectangle

Continue to draw squares in this spiral formation with lengths increasing following the Fibonacci sequence. The result should look something like this (Figure 4.10).

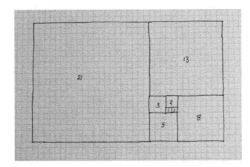

Figure 4.10 Golden rectangles

How many rectangles can children draw? What do they notice about the rectangles? Would it make any difference using larger or smaller squared paper? The children could test this out. If they add sheets of paper together, what is the largest sequence of rectangles they can draw?

Plenary

Can they describe the 'movement' of the rectangles from the centre? Show the children how to draw an arc across a square from one corner to another (Figure 4.11). Starting with the first square, can the children draw a continuous spiral following the outward movement of the rectangles? This is the golden spiral.

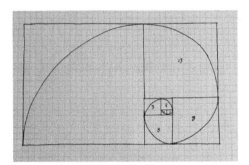

Figure 4.11 The golden spiral

Can children recognise this spiral in nature? Provide photographs or images for them to explore.

Follow-up ideas

Children could use the golden rectangle as a basis for picture frames to display photographs or artwork. These could be made with dowelling, art straws or lolly sticks cut to the lengths of the Fibonacci numbers and stuck on to card or balsa wood.

Children could be set the task of bringing in an image of the golden spiral from nature for homework.

Extension

Children could use their knowledge of how to find the golden ratio to draw their own rectangles where $(a + b)/a = a/b = 1.618$ for the line segments a and b. They could compare to the golden rectangle.

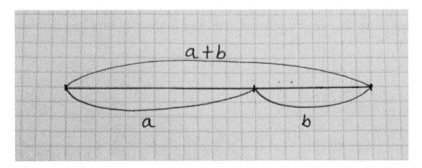

Figure 4.12 The line segments used to derive the golden ratio

Support

Some children could be given pre-cut squares to assemble in the formation of the golden rectangle and supported with calculating the golden ratio.

SYMMETRY IN NATURE

Objective

- To recognise line symmetry in nature and create symmetrical images.

Curriculum links

Mathematics

> **Y2: Geometry:** identify […] line symmetry in a vertical line.
>
> **Y4: Geometry:** identify lines of symmetry in 2-D shapes presented in different orientations, complete a simple symmetric figure with respect to a specific line of symmetry.

Science

> **Y1: Plants:** identify and describe the basic structure of a variety of flowering plants, including trees.
>
> **Y1: Animals including humans:** identify and name a variety of common animals including fish, amphibians, reptiles, birds and mammals.
>
> **Y1: Animals including humans:** describe and compare the structure of a variety of common animals.
>
> **Y3: Plants:** explore the part that flowers play in the life cycle of flowering plants, including pollination, seed formation and seed dispersal.

Background

Children should be introduced to the concept of symmetry before this lesson and given the opportunity to explore symmetry in shapes. They can use mirrors to investigate what it means for a shape to be symmetrical and to identify the lines of symmetry before creating their own symmetrical shapes or images. The following four activities can be completed as part of a carousel activity, as described here where children move around from one activity to the next within one lesson, or they can be completed as four individual activities in separate lessons.

Resources

- Photocopiable: How to make symmetrical animals (p. 54)
- Templates or images of animals
- Colouring pencils/felt-tip pens
- Thin card for symmetrical animals
- A4 paper for pin pictures and symmetrical flowers
- Cartridge paper for string pictures
- Scissors
- Pins
- String
- Poster paints in a range of colours

Introduction

Refer to previous learning on symmetry and remind children about what it means if a shape or image has a line of symmetry. Discuss the idea of symmetry in nature and ask children if they know of any examples. Show children images of animals, insects, and flowers and ask them to point out the lines of symmetry. Discuss why they are symmetrical. Explain to the children that they are going to create their own images to show symmetry in nature. Depending on the age of the children, they can be sent to each activity to work independently from the 'How to …' instruction sheet (see Resources) or teachers can explain each activity to the children first. If other adults are available, they could support different groups. The groups could be rotated until the children have completed all the activities.

Main session

Activity 1: Symmetrical animals

Using the card and following the instructions, children draw their animal and cut it out. Templates of animals can be provided for those less confident at drawing. They can colour and add features using mirrors to ensure both sides are symmetrical. They can then fold their animal and stand it up. Other animals or different sizes of the same animal can be made if time allows.

Figure 4.13 Decorate both sides

Figure 4.14 Completed 3-D animals

Activity 2: Pin pictures

Fold a piece of paper in half and draw half of an image, for example a flower, butterfly or ladybird, along the fold line. Using a safety pin or straight pin put holes in the outline of the flower along the drawn line, keeping fingers out of the way. Using a craft mat or thick piece of fabric underneath should help with this and avoid marking tables. Open out the paper and draw along the line of pinholes to complete the image. A different colour can be used to make the image stand out. Children can then colour and decorate their images.

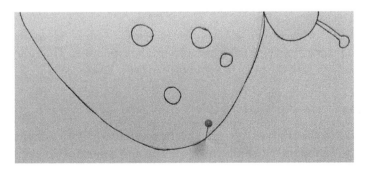

Figure 4.15 Pin pictures

Activity 3: Symmetrical flowers

Fold the paper in half and draw half of a flower along the fold line, as in the activity above. Pre-drawn pictures can be given to younger children. Open out the paper and lay it flat on the table. Using thick felt-tip pens or water-based paints, colour just inside the outline taking care not to colour beyond the fold line. Before the colour dries fold the paper over on top of the image and press down so that the imprint is transferred to the blank part of the page. Open out the paper and see the image reflected across the fold line. Children could colour in the whole image rather than just along the outline if it is easier and fold in the same way to transfer the image.

Figure 4.16 Symmetrical flowers

Activity 4: String pictures

Fold the paper in half. Lay a length of string along the fold line so that some string hangs out from the bottom of the paper. Using poster paint or other thick paint, drop different colours onto one side of the paper. Fold the paper closed making sure the string remains along the fold line. Press down on the paper, at the same time pulling the string up and out to the side so that it is drawn through the paint. Remove the string totally and open the paper to reveal the symmetrical image created. Children can add antennae and outline wings to turn their image into a butterfly or just cut around the shape and display as symmetrical art.

Figure 4.17 String pictures

Plenary

Children can use mirrors to check the symmetry in their pictures. They can also draw a line along the folds to highlight the lines of symmetry in their images.

Follow-up ideas

Children can research the animals they have made particularly if the activity is part of a topic on animals. The 3-D animals can be attached to string and a piece of dowelling and made into puppets or used in story boxes as a stimulus for writing and storytelling. The pin pictures and symmetrical flowers can be used to make cards or framed to make pictures. They can also be attached to string and suspended as mobiles.

Extension

Can children create pictures with more than one line of symmetry and pictures that have rotational symmetry?

Support

Some children may be less confident with drawing the animals and templates can be provided for support. Some younger children may need support with cutting the images and with pushing the pins through the paper. Some children may not be able to follow the 'How to …' sheets so may need the teacher to demonstrate the activity first.

NUMBER PATTERNS

Objective

• To investigate patterns and make general statements about numbers.

Curriculum links

Mathematics

Y1: **Number: number and place value:** (non-statutory guidance) recognise and create repeating patterns with objects and with shapes.

Y2: **Number: number and place value:** (non-statutory guidance) develop further their recognition of patterns within the number system and represent them in different ways, including spatial representations.

Y5: **Number: number and place value:** (non-statutory guidance) recognise and describe linear number sequences […] and find the term-to-term rule.

Y6: **Algebra:** use simple formulae, generate and describe linear number sequences, (non-statutory guidance) use symbols and letters to represent variables and unknowns in mathematical situations that they already understand, such as formulae in mathematics and science, […] generalisations of number patterns.

Science

Working scientifically: supports and extends children's experiences of pattern seeking.

Background

The following activities focus in particular on number patterns. From the earlier activities in this chapter, the children have a developing understanding of pattern in nature and their environment. Finding and understanding patterns gives children a sense of achievement. Teachers can build on this to develop children's understanding of pattern in our number system and how numbers are connected. It is important that children are given opportunities to explore and investigate numbers using physical representations from an early age. Recognising patterns in number helps children to make generalisations based on what they have noticed. Developing the skills of pattern spotting and generalising from an early age better supports children's understanding of algebra.

Activity

Resources

- Cuisenaire® rods
- Large squared paper
- Pencils
- Colouring pencils

Introduction

Remind the children of patterns found in the Fibonacci sequence and how they represented it using Cuisenaire rods. Give the children opportunities to play with the rods and explore the different patterns they can make particularly if teaching this activity to KS1 children who may be using Cuisenaire rods for the first time. They may create patterns such as those seen in Figure 4.18 and should be encouraged to describe their patterns.

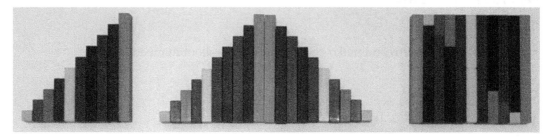

Figure 4.18 Number patterns

Main session

Children can then be set a more focused task of creating specific patterns such as finding all possibilities as in the following activity.

Activity 1: finding possibilities

Choose a purple Cuisenaire rod. Using the other coloured rods, how many different ways can the children make the same length? How can they be sure they have made all the possibilities? Encourage the children to be systematic. If they give values to the rods, what do they notice about the numbers? The children could then choose their own rods to find all possible combinations. Can the children describe what is happening and spot any patterns?

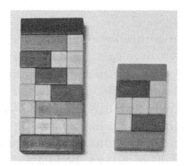

Figure 4.19 Finding possibilities

This activity could be developed further to support children in their understanding of fractions as they build fraction walls and explore equivalency. Older children can use the fraction walls to compare, add and subtract fractions and record their calculations.

Figure 4.20 Fraction walls

Activity 2: Cuisenaire flowers

Show the children the first three patterns in the sequence (Figure 4.21) and ask them to recreate it. What do they notice about the pattern? Can they describe it? Can they make the next flower in the sequence? Can they make a general statement for any number of flowers? What happens if the children join the flowers together as in Figure 4.22? Can they describe how the pattern has changed?

Figure 4.21 Cuisenaire flowers

Figure 4.22 Cuisenaire flowers joined together

Activity 3: Cuisenaire rods

Make a square with the smallest rods. Make the next square with one white rod and four red rods. Make another square with four green rods and two red rods (see Figure 4.23). Can the children describe what is happening as the pattern grows? What will the next square look like? How many rods will there be in the centre and how many will there be around the outside? Can the children make a general statement to describe what would happen for any number of rods?

Figure 4.23 Cuisenaire rods

Examples of this and other activities can be found on the NRICH website (https://nrich. maths.org/).

Plenary

Ask the children to share their patterns and how they have continued the sequence. Discuss their general statements and test them to see if they work. The children could work in pairs to create their own growing patterns and describe how their pattern is changing.

Follow-up ideas

The children could use the rods to make triangle numbers and explore the pattern. They could investigate what happens when two consecutive triangle numbers are added. They could follow this up by investigating square numbers and describing the pattern.

Extension

Older children could be asked to make general statements for any number in the sequences and describe the nth term. Younger children could be introduced to the concept of algebra using the Cuisenaire rods to record 2red + 1yellow = 1blue, which can be written as 2r + 1y = 1b. The image in Figure 4.24 would support this calculation.

Figure 4.24 Early algebra with Cuisenaire

Support

Some children may need to be supported to recognise the pattern and may need to build up more shapes before they can see what is happening. They may need prompts and further questioning from the teacher before they can describe the pattern.

3-D SHAPE BUBBLES

Objective

- To use knowledge of the properties of 3-D shapes to reason about shapes.

Curriculum links

Mathematics

Y2: Geometry: identify and describe properties of 3-D shapes, including the number of edges, vertices and faces.

Y3: Geometry: [...] make 3-D shapes using modelling materials; recognise 3-D shapes in different orientations and describe them.

Y6: Geometry: recognise, describe and build simple 3-D shapes, including building nets.

Science

Y3: Light: notice that light is reflected from surfaces.

Y6: Light: (non-statutory guidance) extend their experience of light by looking at a range of phenomena including rainbows, colours on soap bubbles [...].

Living things and their habitats: No direct links but extends learning and knowledge of natural structures such as honeycomb and wasps' nests.

D&T

Technical knowledge

KS1: build structures, exploring how they can be made stronger, stiffer and more stable.

KS2: apply their knowledge of how to strengthen, stiffen and reinforce more complex structures.

Background

We live in a world in which we are surrounded by 3-D shapes that require us to negotiate, operate, manipulate, reason, visualise and problem-solve. Practical experiences help to develop our spatial abilities so that we can navigate our world more easily. It is important that we also provide children with practical experiences and opportunities to reason about the shapes around them. The following activity provides such an opportunity as children make 3-D shapes and investigate what happens when they combine them with bubbles.

Activity

Resources

- Variety of bubble wands
- Plastic or art straws

- Hair grips or pipe cleaners
- Washing-up liquid
- Sugar or glycerine
- Bowl of water deep enough to submerge the cube
- Recipe for bubble mixture:
  - Mix one part washing-up liquid to four parts water. Add two teaspoons of sugar or glycerine and stir well

Introduction

What do we know about bubbles? What shapes are they? What shapes are the bubble wands? Predict what will happen if we blow bubbles from a square shape, triangular shape, etc.? Test various bubble wands and notice what happens. What kind of bubbles could we make with a cube?

Main session

The children could do some research to find out how bubbles are made and why they are more easily formed in soapy water than ordinary water. Use straws and hair grips or pipe cleaners to make a cube (see Building with triangles activity in Chapter 10). Straws can be cut to make smaller cubes or left as their original length.

Mix the bubble mixture according to the recipe above. Test the solution and add more washing-up liquid if the bubbles do not form properly. Give each group a bowl of bubble mixture. Be prepared for some drips on the tables. This can be carried out as a demonstration to the whole class if preferred.

The children can submerge their cubes in their bowls and carefully remove without bursting any bubbles. What do the children notice about the shape of the bubbles? What shapes can they see? What colours can they see? What causes the colours in the bubbles? The children could research this and what happens to the light around bubbles. Investigate light reflection and refraction. They could also investigate why bubbles burst. What would happen if they poked the bubble with a wet stick or straw? Can they explain this?

Can the children predict the bubble shapes made from other 3-D shapes such as a tetrahedron? Immerse in water and investigate. Try blowing the bubbles to see what happens.

Figure 4.25 Making bubbles with a tetrahedron

Plenary

Discuss with the children what they have found out from their investigations with shapes and bubbles. The children could present their findings in groups. Which shape made the biggest bubble?

Follow-up ideas

Children could investigate making a spherical shape from pipe cleaners and test this to see if they could make bubbles. What other ways can they make bubbles?

Extension

Children could explore light reflection and refraction in more detail.

Support

Some children may need support to make their 3-D shapes and to carry out research about bubbles.

CARGOES

Objective

- To investigate loading of planes, ships and lorries.
- To use symmetrical patterns to help to load cargo successfully.
- This activity can be used as a balancing activity or the children could build the apparatus first and test it before giving it to younger children and helping them to investigate.

Curriculum links

Mathematics

Y2: Geometry: identify […] line symmetry in a vertical line.

Y4: Geometry: identify lines of symmetry in 2-D shapes presented in different orientations, complete a simple symmetric figure with respect to a specific line of symmetry.

Science

Y3: Forces and magnets: No direct links but introduces the concept of weight as a force.

Y5: Forces: No direct links but reinforces work on levers.

Background

Anyone who has ever sat in a small boat knows the importance of balancing the cargo. Too many people on one side can cause the boat to capsize. The same balancing act is needed in aircraft, where the cargo (or passengers) must be distributed evenly from side-to-side and from front-to-back. On flights with more than one destination, it is not unusual for passengers to be re-seated after the first stop, if significant numbers have disembarked. Ships and planes must be carefully loaded in order to keep them balanced. A badly loaded ship will be more at risk from capsize in choppy waters and a badly loaded aircraft might never successfully take off or land, even if the pilot was able to fly it without crashing! Symmetrical loading of identical mass cargo is the key; however, most cargoes consist of a variety of sizes and masses so that consideration must be paid to the arrangement. This idea is the basis for turning moments, which are studied in KS3 science. This activity could be linked to the 'Payloads' activity (Chapter 9).

Resources

- Photocopiable: Vehicle shapes 1 and 2 (pp. 55, 56)
- Assorted cargo: small toys, building bricks, modelling clay, paperclips etc.
- Scales (balance)
- Polystyrene to make floating models

Introduction

Discuss the problems of loading cargo, or passengers, onto a boat. Ask what will happen if the passengers all sit on one side, or if all the cargo is loaded on to the back. If necessary, this can be demonstrated using a model boat and some suitable passengers. The children should be able to suggest suitable arrangements to keep the boat level. Introduce the idea of balancing from side-to-side and also from front-to-back (fore-to-aft/bow-to-stern). Extend the ideas to loading planes.

Show the apparatus and explain the task.

Main session

Children investigate loading the ship and plane shapes with a variety of cargoes. The ship or aircraft shape should be laminated, cut out carefully and allowed to hang freely from a hook, the black dot shows the position of the hole for hanging. The children should record the weight of the cargo and its position. Patterns should emerge: symmetrical loading is best if everything weighs the same; otherwise, it is best to put heavier things nearer the middle or central pivot point.

Plenary

Discuss the children's findings. What do they notice about the loading patterns? Is symmetrical loading always a good idea? Find out whether any children were able to find a link between weight and distance from the central point (weight has more effect on the balance the further it is from the central point).

Follow-up ideas

Repeat the activity but using polystyrene cut-outs floating in water (Figure 4.26). Choose a suitable cargo and ask the children to load the shapes so they do not tip over. Aircraft shapes can be used in this activity too with the water playing the role of air.

Investigate catamarans and trimarans (Figure 4.27) and the role the extra hulls play in stability.

Children could research how large cruise ships can remain as stable as possible in rough conditions.

Figure 4.26 Balanced, symmetrical cargo on polystyrene shapes

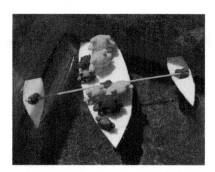

Figure 4.27 A trimaran – the extra hulls add stability to the shape so loading of cargo can be less symmetrical

Extension

Introduce moments and show how to calculate them (moment = weight of object × distance from pivot). The children can weigh the cargo and decide on a suitable arrangement using moments, before they use the apparatus. Information on calculating moments can be found in any KS3 physics text book or on-line.

Support

Use cargoes that all have the same mass so that symmetrical loading is the only factor involved.

How to make symmetrical animals

You will need:

A4 thin card

scissors

drawing pencil

felt tips or colouring pencils

cut out images or wooden templates of animals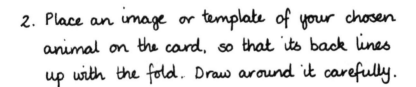

1. Fold the card in half.

2. Place an image or template of your chosen animal on the card, so that its back lines up with the fold. Draw around it carefully.

3. Keeping the card folded, cut along the lines you've drawn. You will cut through both layers at the same time. Do not cut along the fold.

4. Open the cut out shape and decorate both halves. Remember to decorate them symmetrically!

5. Refold the card and stand your symmetrical animal upright.

Figure 4.28

Vehicle shapes 1

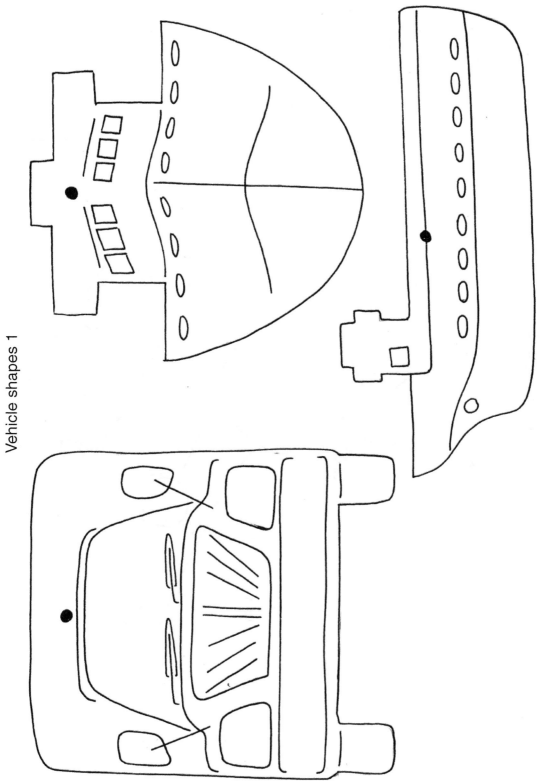

Figure 4.29

Vehicle shapes 2

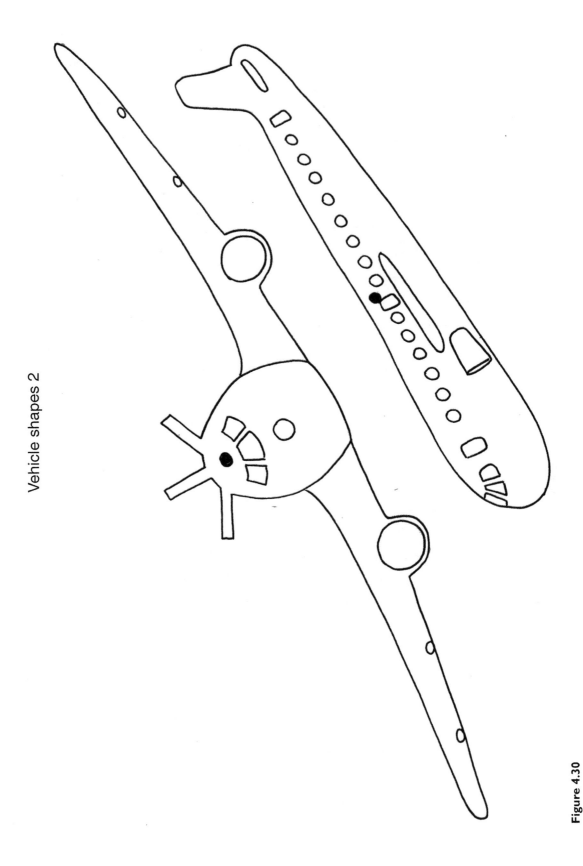

Figure 4.30

CHAPTER 5

A to B

5.1 Egg race

5.2 Defying gravity

5.3 Post a crisp

5.4 Animal antics

5.5 Is fastest best?

5.6 Cable cars and lifts

OVERVIEW

The activities in this chapter focus on the problem of moving something somewhere. The 'something' may be living or non-living and the mode of transport could be self-propulsion, use of natural phenomena such as wind and water or using mechanical means. In moving something, carriers need to consider speed, cost and route; how the 'something' is to be carried; whether it is fragile or likely to move around in transit; and how heavy it is.

HEALTH AND SAFETY

Care must be taken if tools are to be used. Have a designated sawing/drilling bench, which is supervised at all times.

Be aware of food allergies.

Have a defined test area where the children can test vehicles and take measurements.

When launching seeds, choose an area well away from cars and pedestrians who could be damaged by flying structures. Walk upwind as far as possible before launching. Do not underestimate the success of these seeds!

Attach all pulleys firmly to stable and strong supports such as heavy tables. If attaching the pulleys to shelves, make sure the shelves are themselves firmly attached to the wall/bookcase. If you have to use tape to attach pulleys, keep the loads as light as possible to avoid injury if the tape fails.

EGG RACE

Objective

- To build a vehicle to transport an egg.
- To consider various means of propulsion.

Curriculum links

Mathematics

> **Y2: Measurement:** choose and use appropriate standard units to estimate and measure length/height in any direction (m/cm) and mass (kg/g) […] to the nearest appropriate unit, using rulers, scales.
> **Y5: Measurement:** use all four operations to solve problems involving measure […] using decimal notation, including scaling.

Science

> **Y2: Uses of everyday materials:** identify and compare the suitability of everyday materials, including wood, metal, plastic, […] paper and cardboard for particular uses.
> **Y3: Forces and magnets:** compare how things move on different surfaces.
> **Y5: Properties and changes of materials:** give reasons, based on evidence from comparative and fair tests, for the particular uses of everyday materials, including metals, wood and plastic.
> **Y5: Forces:** identify the effects of air resistance […] and friction, that act between moving surfaces.

D&T

Technical knowledge

> **KS1:** build structures, exploring how they can be made stronger, stiffer and more stable.
> **KS1:** explore and use mechanisms [for example, levers, sliders, wheels and axels], in their

products.

KS2: apply their understanding of how to strengthen, stiffen and reinforce more complex structures.

KS2: understand and use mechanical systems in their products [for example, gears, pulleys, cams, levers and linkages].

KS2: understand and use electrical systems in their products [for example, series circuits incorporating switches, bulbs, buzzers and motors].

Background

The Great Egg Race was a popular television series in the 1980s. Teams of inventors built mechanical contraptions from everyday materials to solve a variety of problems. Initially, the contraptions moved eggs, but later on other challenges were introduced. The contestants researched, planned, built, tested and evaluated their designs following the Design Cycle now used in primary D&T lessons. Some episodes are available on the internet. Many of the challenges are simple enough to be adapted for primary-age children. In this activity, the challenge is to move an egg or suitable substitute (a ping pong ball, ball of modelling clay etc.) across the playground.

Resources

- Junk materials for building: wood, card, paper, dowel, cotton reels, string
- Construction sets e.g. Lego®, if required
- Tape
- Glue
- Materials that can be used to produce a means of propulsion: elastic bands, balloons, old wind-up toys, electric motors (if appropriate)
- Tools: saws, scissors, hammers, nails and drills (depending on age and skills)
- Paper and pencils for planning and drawing designs
- Eggs or suitable substitutes

Introduction

Introduce the challenge and show the resources available. Remind children of the need to plan and test designs as they work. Encourage them to draw plans of their contraptions and to record the changes they make.

Discuss means of propulsion. You may decide that the vehicles will be wind-powered, so discuss sails and fins. If mechanical means are to be used, demonstrate how a balloon (Figure 5.7) or twisted elastic band can be used to move a vehicle (Figure 5.8). If electric motors are to be used, remind children about gears and how to make a suitable circuit (Figure 5.9). To simplify things, old wind-up toys can be cannibalised for their mechanisms.

If appropriate, show part of one of *The Great Egg Race* episodes, emphasise the planning stage and point out how the inventors test various components to check the properties.

Figure 5.7 A balloon-powered vehicle

Figure 5.8 An elastic band-powered vehicle

Figure 5.9 A geared motor attached to the chassis of a wheeled vehicle

Main session

In teams, the children work to solve the challenge. This might be spread over several sessions or be a whole day event.

If there is time, use one session to explore means of propulsion. Children can investigate propulsion by wind, twisted elastic band, balloon, electric motor and wind-up mechanisms.

Encourage proper planning and designing. Children should produce design specifications and plans before they start building.

Plenary

Contraptions are put to the test and scores are awarded for a successful journey as well as for speed, good design and team work.

Follow-up ideas

The children could evaluate their designs and suggest improvements.

If the contraptions are still in one piece and functional after the trial, they could be used for a second journey over a different distance or terrain.

This would work very well as a STEM/Science Week challenge that the children work on at home with parents and carers. They could bring their finished contraptions to school at the end of the week for a grand, public trial.

Extension

Add a score for accuracy: the egg must be delivered to a certain point at the end of the journey.

Give the children a budget and 'sell' the building materials to them. This should encourage sensible use of resources and more thought about the final design before construction takes place. Points can be awarded for teams coming in under budget.

Support

Provide a kit of parts that can be assembled to produce a suitable vehicle. This could be made from construction kits rather than junk materials.

DEFYING GRAVITY (SEED DISPERSAL)

Objective

- To investigate methods of seed dispersal.
- To study the effects of changing structure or method on distance travelled.

Curriculum links

Mathematics

Y2: **Measurement:** choose and use appropriate standard units to estimate and measure length/height in any direction (m/cm) and mass (kg/g) [...] to the nearest appropriate unit, using rulers, scales.

Y4: **Measurement:** find the area of a rectilinear shape by counting squares.

Y5: **Measurement:** calculate and compare the area of rectangles [...] and estimate the area of irregular shapes.

Y2: **Statistics:** interpret and construct simple tables.

Y5: **Statistics:** interpret and present discrete and continuous data using appropriate graphical methods.

Science

Y1: **Plants:** describe the basic structure of a variety of common flowering plants, including trees.

Y3: **Plants:** explore the part that flowers play in the life cycle of flowering plants, including [...] seed dispersal.

Y5: **Forces:** identify the effects of air resistance [...].

Y6: **Evolution and inheritance:** identify how animals and plants are adapted to suit their environment in different ways and that adaptation may lead to evolution.

Background

Many plants use wind to disperse their seeds. There are two ways that plants do this: they make such tiny, light seeds that they are easily blown away by the wind or they produce seeds with some sort of wing or parachute, which allows them to float on wind currents and not simply fall straight down. Other plants use animals to help move seeds around. The animals may have to eat a tasty fruit or collect and bury a nut. Other seeds have hooks on the outer coat, which can get caught up in fur as the animal brushes past. Some plants move their seeds by explosion when the seed pods break open with great energy, firing the seeds out and away from the parent plant. Seeds are also distributed by water with large but buoyant seeds being dropped into the sea or a river.

All these methods of dispersal are open to investigation and ideas can be found in many science books. In this activity, the focus is on wind dispersal because of the vast array of different structures and methods that the plants use to harness the wind's power.

Resources

- Examples of wind-dispersed seeds: sycamore, lime, hornbeam, dandelion, ash
- Small seeds e.g. mustard, cress or radish
- Junk materials: card, paper, toothpicks, skewers, fabric, tissue paper, lolly sticks
- Tape
- Glue
- Rulers
- Squared paper
- Scales (balance)

Introduction

Show the children the seeds and demonstrate how they twirl and float downwards. The greater the height from which the seeds are dropped, the better the effect. If possible, show a film of wind-dispersed seeds. Point out that the longer a seed can stay aloft, fighting the pull of gravity, the further it can be blown by a breeze.

Discuss why plants need to move their seeds and what advantages and disadvantages the seeds might gain from the move.

Drop a mustard, cress or radish seed and show how it just falls to the floor, even in a breeze. Challenge the children to make a structure to fix to the seed so that it can become a wind-dispersed seed. Remind children that the key to success is to keep the seed in the air as long as possible.

Main session

Using the materials provided, and plenty of trial and improvement, the children design and make 'wings' for their seed.

Once they have a suitable design, the children should try to calculate the surface area of the wing. They can do this by measuring the sides if the wing is rectangular, or by drawing round the wing on 1 cm squared paper and counting the squares, for odd shaped wings. They should also weigh the whole structure.

Test the seeds outside by dropping them from a predetermined height and measuring how far they travel. Avoid throwing the seeds. This is best done on a windy day because the junk structures may be fairly heavy. Record the distance and, if time permits, have second and third trials in order to take account of any gusts or calm patches.

If you cannot get outside to do the test, or if there is no wind, it can be done inside but then it is more helpful to time how long the seeds take to fall rather than how far they fly.

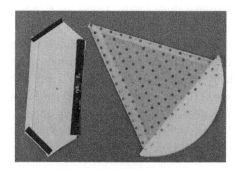

Figure 5.10 Two successful seed designs

Plenary

Collate the results in a table showing the mass of the structure, the area of the wing and the distance flown/time to fall. Are there any patterns? Did light structures always out-perform heavy ones, regardless of wing area? Was a large wing area the key to long flight?

If appropriate, discuss how the seeds 'evolved' as the children tested and altered their designs. Link this to variation and adaptation.

Follow-up ideas

Weigh the real wind-dispersed seeds and measure their wing surface areas. Look at the ratio of weight to surface area and then compare with the weight to surface area ratios of the children's seeds. Is there a correlation?

Look at the motion of the sycamore and ash seeds. They spin like a helicopter. Can the children make a seed that does the same? They will need to investigate wing shape and orientation.

Research gliding animals such as flying fish and flying squirrels. They increase their surface area in order to 'fly'. The children could try to find out how.

Extension

Plot scatter graphs of the data (surface area against distance or weight against distance) and look for any correlations.

Challenge the children to use a heavier seed. Ask them to consider what changes they should make to their designs.

Support

Provide some pre-formed wings for the children to choose from. These could all be the same shape but made from different materials or could all be made from the same material but in different shapes and sizes. This reduces the number of variables.

POST A CRISP

Objective

- To design a package to protect a very fragile item as it travels through the postal system.
- To consider the size limitations and cost of parcel postage.

Curriculum links

Mathematics

Y2: Measurement: choose and use appropriate standard units to estimate and measure length/height in any direction (m/cm) and mass (kg/g) […] to the nearest appropriate unit, using rulers, scales.

Y2: Measurement: solve simple problems in a practical context involving addition and subtraction of money […].

Science

> **Y2: Uses of everyday materials:** identify and compare the suitability of a variety of everyday materials [...] for particular uses.
> **Y3: Forces and magnets:** notice that some forces need contact between two objects [...].
> **Y5: Properties and changes of materials:** give reasons, based on evidence from comparative and fair tests, for the particular uses of everyday materials [...].

Background

From the moment it is dropped into a post box or mail bag, a parcel faces a hostile environment of contact forces. Heavier parcels may land on top of it, the parcel may be dropped or jarred and it may have to be squashed through a small letter box. While it is possible to post fragile items successfully, this activity exposes the fragile potato crisp to the rigours of the normal service for letters.

Resources

- Potato crisps or other fragile food: savoury biscuits, thin chocolate
- A selection of commercially available packaging: padded envelopes, cardboard boxes, reinforced envelopes
- Junk materials: card, paper, foil, bubble wrap, cotton wool, plastic bags, polystyrene packaging chips
- Scissors
- Tape
- Glue
- Parcel size information and costs
- A5 envelopes
- A selection of stamps
- Photocopiable: Posting guide (enlarge to A3 size) (p. 73)

Introduction

Put one crisp in an ordinary envelope and post it to yourself. It should arrive thoroughly crushed.

Show the crushed crisp to the children and ask why it got damaged on its journey. Discuss the forces to which it might have been exposed.

Ask the children for ideas about better packaging. Show some examples of protective envelopes and, if possible, let the children take them apart to see what is inside. Discuss how the materials protect the contents of the envelope.

Explain the task: to send a crisp through the post without it getting damaged. Remind children that there are costs associated with posting packages and that the bigger the parcel, the more it costs. Show them the size limits for first- and second-class letters, and the costs of parcels that are too big to count as letters. If appropriate, set a budget for postage.

Main session

Children investigate the materials on offer and design their own packaging for the crisp.

If resources and time allow, the children can test their packaging ideas by wrapping up crisps and subjecting them to damaging situations such as forcing them through a small letter box, or dropping a heavier parcel on top of them.

Once the final package design is agreed, it should be assembled, with the crisp inside, and posted. Provide Post Office postage-cost information and stamps for the children to 'buy'. The parcels should be weighed correctly and the size checked as it would be in a Post Office.

Address and post the parcels.

Plenary

If the postage costs have been calculated correctly, and all parcels posted at the same time and the same place, then they should arrive back at about the same time. The children should open their own packages carefully and extract the crisp.

With luck some crisps will have survived their journey better than others. Discuss the successful packages. How have the children protected the crisp from knocks and crushing? Are there any similarities in the designs of the successful packages? What materials were best at protecting the crisp? Try to produce a design for the perfect package.

Figure 5.11 Opening the envelope!

Consider the cost. Were the successful packages always the most expensive to post? Could the weight and size be reduced without compromising crisp safety?

Follow-up ideas

Try to reduce packaging and cost successfully using the knowledge gained from the first posting.

Examine the packaging materials that come with fragile items such as computers and china. Can the children identify the shock-absorbing components?

Discuss environmentally friendly packaging. Much packaging is plastic-based. How could we produce biodegradable packaging that still works? Children could research on-line to find out what exists.

Extension

Use items with a complex 3-D shape such as a Pringle. This adds an extra layer of difficulty to the packaging design.

Give children a budget for the packaging as well as the postage. They should design carefully so that they only buy the resources they need.

Support

Choose a less fragile object to post, for example a thin biscuit.

Give the children a small box or envelope in which to pack their crisp. They can think about how to cushion the crisp but need not worry about the integrity of the outermost packaging.

ANIMAL ANTICS

Objective

- To design a crate for shipping a live animal safely and humanely.
- To work with large weights and volumes.
- To make scale models.

Curriculum links

Mathematics

> **Y2: Measurement:** choose and use appropriate standard units to estimate and measure length/height in any direction (m/cm) and mass (kg/g) […] to the nearest appropriate unit, using rulers, scales.
> **Y2: Statistics:** interpret and construct simple tables.
> **Y3: Number: multiplication and division:** solve problems […] involving multiplication and division, including positive integer scaling problems (for example, 4 times as high).

Science

> **Y1: Animals, including humans:** identify and name a variety of common animals that are carnivores, herbivores and omnivores.
> **Y2: Animals, including humans:** find out about and describe the basic needs of animals for survival.
> **Y3: Animals, including humans:** identify that animals need the right types and amount of nutrition and that they cannot make their own food.

D&T

Technical knowledge

> **KS1:** build structures, exploring how they can be made stronger, stiffer and more stable.
> **KS2:** apply their understanding of how to strengthen, stiffen and reinforce more complex structures.

Background

Zoos and wildlife parks often ship animals around. For example, a male tiger may be moved from the zoo where it was born to another one, halfway around the world, where it can be used in a breeding programme. Moving live animals requires specialist knowledge and equipment and very large crates!

Resources

- Photocopiable: Animal cards (pp. 74, 75): these can just be used as picture cards, or the data sheet can be copied on to the back of the picture sheet to produce cards with a picture and relevant data.
- Access to the internet and reference books
- Masking tape
- Squared paper and isometric paper, if available
- Rulers and metre sticks or wheel
- Scales (balance)
- Card
- Wood (balsa wood is best)
- Scissors or saws
- Glue

Introduction

Explain the task. A zoo wants to ship some animals elsewhere and needs to have suitable crates to put them in. Animals will need room to move a little, and to lie down and stand up (if they do that). There must be a way to feed and water them safely and the crates must allow light and air in.

Ask the children what sort of measurements they will need in order to be able to design a crate. What other information needs to be taken into account?

For simplicity, these animals will be moved by road and the journey will only take a day. The crates can be lifted onto the transport vehicle by a suitably sized crane.

Using tape, mark out a rectangle about 6 m long and 2.5 m wide. An African elephant could probably just fit inside this rectangle. This will give the children some idea about the dimensions they are dealing with. Explain why they will only be making a scale model!

Hand out animal cards to the children or let them choose their own animal.

Figure 5.12 Children marking out a 6 m × 2.5 m rectangle

Main session

Children use the internet or reference books to find out about their animal. They will need to know an average value for height and length as well as a weight for the animal. They should also find out about diet and estimate how much food the animal will need on its journey and whether it will also need a water supply. Data regarding width of animals are hard to locate, so the children could design a crate to fit on a standard road trailer, which is limited to a maximum width of 2.55 m in the UK.

The children design a crate, thinking about the size and weight of the animal. They should add information to their design about the sizes of the crate, the materials they would use to build it and how they will feed the animal; will there be a hatch or a manger or will the food hang from the roof?

If you have isometric paper, the children can draw a 3-D view of their crate.

Once designed, the children can make a scale model of their design. They will need to work out the sizes for the scale model, so use a suitable scale depending on the children's mathematical ability. A tenth scale model will be fairly easy to calculate. The model can be made from card or wood as appropriate.

Plenary

Children exhibit their model and designs. They tell their peers about their design and how it takes into account the needs of both the animal and the keepers looking after it.

Follow-up ideas

Look for news reports of animal transport. Ask at the local zoo for pictures of the crates they use to transport animals.

Ask a zoologist or vet to talk to the children about transporting animals safely. This could include transporting domestic animals and pets.

Extension

Choose less common animals to transport so that the children will have to do more in-depth research.

Suggest a more complex scale factor. Ask the children to scale the weight too and then to use modelling clay of the correct weight to make a scale model of the animal to fit in the crate.

Supply model animals and ask the children to make the crate on the same scale as the model. This will involve measuring the model, working out the scale compared to a real animal and then scaling their shipping crate by the same factor.

Support

Provide the animal data, with sizes and weights in suitable units and rounded to make calculations easier (see Resources).

Provide model animals for the children to measure. The children can design their crate to suit the model.

IS FASTEST BEST?

Objective

- To learn how to calculate speed from distance and time measurements.
- To investigate different methods of producing movement in a clockwork toy.

Curriculum links

Mathematics

Y2: **Measurement:** choose and use appropriate standard units to estimate and measure length […] in any direction (m/cm) […] to the nearest appropriate unit, using rulers.

Y3: **Measurement:** compare durations of events [for example, to calculate the time taken by particular events or tasks].

Y2: **Statistics:** interpret and construct simple tables.

Y5: **Measurement**: use all four operations to solve problems involving measure […] using decimal notation, including scaling.

Science

Y3: **Forces and magnets:** compare how things move on different surfaces.

Y5: **Forces:** recognise that some mechanisms, including […] gears, allow a small force to have a greater effect.

D&T

Technical knowledge

KS1: explore and use mechanisms [for example, […] wheels and axels] in their products.

KS2: understand and use mechanical systems in their products [for example, gears […]].

Background

This activity is a useful introduction to the uses of gears. Most toy motors spin very fast (wind up a clockwork car, hold it in the air and watch the wheels). However, a fast motor is not always a strong motor. Using gears, which will slow down the spin, also increases the torque, or strength, of the motor. So, assuming all toys have a similar type of motor mechanism inside, the slower ones have probably got some gears too, making them slow but strong and able to pull a heavier load than the fast vehicles. If you can, take the vehicles apart and look for the gear wheels.

Resources

- A selection of cars and trains that are powered in different ways: wind-up, pull-back, balloon, battery, pneumatic
- Timers

- 100 g or 50 g masses
- Measuring tape or metre sticks
- Calculators

Introduction

Show the different vehicles to the children and ask how they are powered. Set the vehicles in motion and estimate which ones go furthest and which go fastest.

Explain that the children are going to measure the speed of each vehicle and the maximum distance it can travel without having to be re-activated.

Main session

The children record the time each vehicle covers a set distance (1 m is usually sufficient). Using a calculator, they can calculate the average speed of the vehicle over the distance (speed = distance ÷ time).

The children can also measure the maximum distance the vehicle can travel (avoid using the battery-powered toys for this part) and record this.

Once the children have completed this task, explain that the vehicle needs to carry a passenger or pull a load represented by the 50 g or 100 g masses. The children then repeat their measurements for each vehicle now with a load of 50 g or 100 g. They should also record the maximum weight that the vehicle can pull.

Plenary

Collate the results from the two activities. Were the fastest vehicles able to move once they had a passenger? Can the children think of an explanation?

If appropriate, discuss the role of the gears, which can slow down the spin from motors and therefore give the vehicle more power.

This is not a fair test as the vehicles are all different sizes and shapes. A discussion about the problems of comparison can be useful here. If possible, try to find at least two vehicles that weigh approximately the same amount and are about the same size so that some comparisons can be made.

Follow-up ideas

The children can design and make trailers for the vehicles or alter the structure of the vehicle to allow more passengers to travel.

The children could try to link two vehicles with similar speeds together. What happens to the speed and how effective is the double vehicle at carrying a load? This can be linked to examples of trains when there are two engines used to pull the train.

Try using bath toys in a paddling pool instead. Most of these toys have a wind-up mechanism but they use different propulsion methods (fins spin, tails flap etc.), which can be investigated.

Extension

Not all toy vehicles run in straight lines. Challenge the children to work out the total distance travelled if the vehicle is one that travels in a curve.

The speed calculation used in the activity gives the average speed over the distance but most wind-up type toys will start fast and slow down so the children could try to measure the speed at different points on the journey and show how it changes.

Support

Instead of calculating speed, fix a time and measure how far each vehicle travels in the time. Explain that the fastest vehicle will travel the furthest in the time. Use a long piece of paper as the 'track' and draw a mark to show the point that each vehicle reached in the time. This provides a clear visual summary of the results.

Alternatively, the children can measure the time taken to travel a particular distance. The times can then be ordered to show which vehicle took the shortest time (the fastest vehicle) and which the longest. Use a timer that measures only whole seconds.

CABLE CARS AND LIFTS

Objective

- To investigate the functions of pulleys.

Curriculum links

Mathematics

> **Y2: Measurement:** choose and use appropriate standard units to estimate and measure length/height in any direction (m/cm) and mass (kg/g) […] to the nearest appropriate unit, using rulers, scales.

Science

> **Y5: Forces:** recognise that some mechanisms including […] pulleys allow a smaller force to have a greater effect.

D&T

Technical knowledge

> **KS1:** explore and use mechanisms [for example, […] wheels and axels] in their products.
> **KS2:** understand and use mechanical systems in their products [for example, gears, pulleys […]].

Background

Lifts and cable cars are machines used to move things up; either to the top of a building or to the summit of a mountain. The machinery that powers the lift or cable car is situated at one point and the force produced to move the load up is transmitted from the engine to the load via pulleys and cables. Pulleys are simple machines; their job is as force converters. For example, pulleys can change the direction of a force: a downwards pull becomes an upwards lift and a pull to the left becomes movement to the right. Pulleys can also increase the power of a force. This is not demonstrated in this activity, which serves as a simple introduction to pulleys and their properties.

Resources

- Pulleys: these can be home made from cotton reels on pencils (Figure 5.13)
- Wood blocks or pegs to hold the pulley mechanism
- String

- Clamps
- Suitable cargo

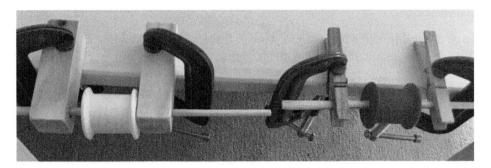

Figure 5.13 Two home-made pulley systems

Introduction

Most children will have travelled in a lift and some may also have been on a cable car or chair lift. Discuss why they used the lift/cable car. Was it easier than walking? Why? What was doing the work? Children who have travelled in cable cars or chair lifts may have seen part of the machinery that is involved so ask them for details or show a picture and discuss what the 'big wheel' is doing. Cable cars have huge pulley wheels at both ends of the line and these are usually visible.

Main session

Challenge the children to bridge a void between two tables or lift a load to the top of the bookshelves using pulleys.

They will need to decide how long the string should be, where the pulleys should be located and how the load can be attached. They may want to have several cars on their system and they should think about whether the pulley wheels should be vertical or horizontal.

It is very important that the pulleys are firmly attached to their supports and the string running through them is fairly taut. If this is hard to maintain then make sure that the loads carried are very light so that there is no risk of total collapse of the system.

Once the cable cars or lifts are working, give the children some cargo that needs to be moved from one end of the cable to the other. They can decide how to load it. It may need several journeys, or several cars, to get it all to the end point. Too heavy a load can result in failure of the lift or cable car and this is a useful discussion point. Children will probably have noticed the 'maximum load' labels in lifts and cable cars.

Plenary

The children can demonstrate their models.

Discuss how the pulley is changing the direction of the force: ask them to show in which direction they are pulling the string and to demonstrate how the load can be travelling the opposite way.

Follow-up ideas

Motorise a lift using a small, geared model motor. Use a suitable electric circuit with a switch to control the motor and stop the lift at various points.

Add extra pulleys to a lift to show how multiple-pulley systems can make lifting heavy loads easier.

Extension

Challenge the children to add a second stage to their cable car: so it first crosses a valley and then goes up a mountain. If making a lift, perhaps it could go up and then across like the one in Mr Wonka's chocolate factory.

Ask the children to make their own pulleys from junk materials rather than using ready-made ones. They should think about how to keep the string in place on the wheel and how to allow the wheel to turn freely.

Support

Cut string to length so that it will reach across the void or up the wall and back again without too much slack.

Fasten the pulleys in place for the children and ask them to sort out how to loop the string around in order to transport the cable car.

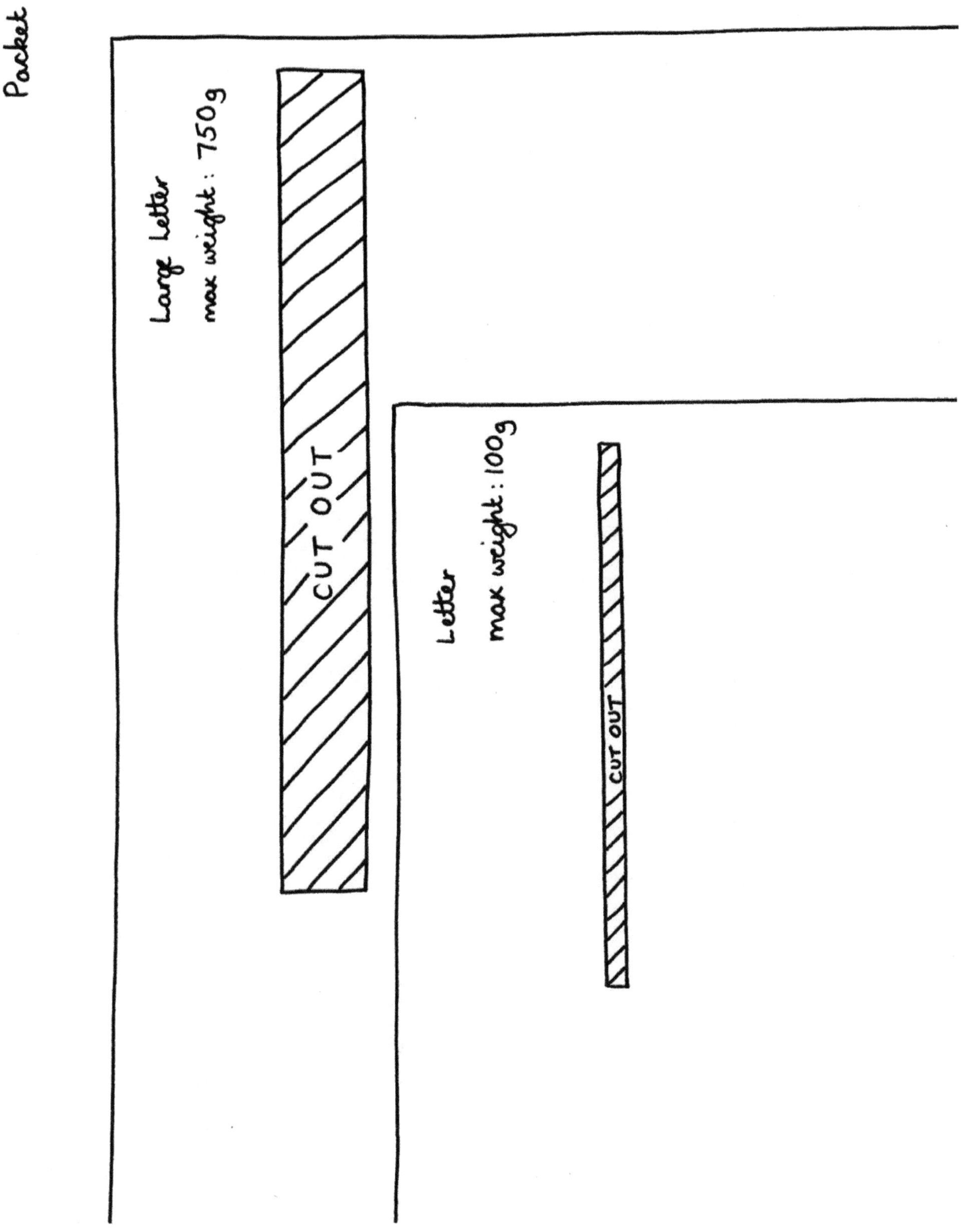

Packet

Large Letter
max weight: 750g

CUT OUT

Letter
max weight: 100g

CUT OUT

Figure 5.14 Posting guide

Figure 5.15 Animal cards (front)

Rhino

Height: 2 m
Length: 4 m
Weight: 20 00 kg

Elephant

Height: 4 m
Length: 6½ m
Weight: 50 00 kg

Tiger

Height: 1 m
Length: 2 m
Weight: 200 kg

Lion

Height: 1 m
Length: 2 m
Weight: 200 kg

Bear

Height: 1 m (standing on all paws)
Length: 2½ m
Weight: 800 kg

Giraffe

Height: 5 m
Length: 1½ m
Weight: 1000 kg

Moose

Height: 2 m
Length: 3 m
Weight: 800 kg

Hippo

Height: 1½ m
Length: 3 m
Weight: 2000 kg

Figure 5.16 Animal cards (back)

CHAPTER 6

Plant magic

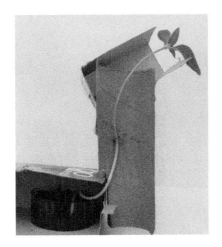

6.1 Pea mazes

6.2 Living walls

6.3 Meet a tree

6.4 Grow a meal

6.5 Plants for building

6.6 Sunflower race

OVERVIEW

Plants are very versatile; they form the basis of a human diet and can also provide shelter for humans. Plant products such as paper and fabrics are used in everyday life. Of course, as plants photosynthesise they produce the oxygen humans need. Without plants, humans would not survive. These activities focus on plants, the conditions they need to grow well and their uses and hopefully give some insight into their beauty and magic!

HEALTH AND SAFETY

Hands should be washed thoroughly after any gardening activities.

Consider the choice of plants. Use ones that are safe to touch and that are less likely to cause hay fever. When choosing edible plants, check for any food allergies.

Any work in woodland involves hazards such as tripping over fallen branches, particles in the eye, cuts and bruises from the rough and broken wood that might be around. Take appropriate precautions. Avoid woodland work on very windy days as branches may be at risk of falling.

Testing materials is potentially dangerous, so ensure children wear goggles and gloves. If in any doubt, do the tests as a demonstration.

Supervise use of hammers and nails. If children are to go into any structures they have made, the structures need to be checked carefully to ensure that they are solidly built and will not collapse.

PEA MAZES

Objective

- To demonstrate that plants grow towards the light.

Curriculum links

Mathematics

Y1: Measurement: compare, describe and solve practical problems for lengths and heights [for example, long/short, longer/shorter, tall/short, double/half].

Y2: Measurement: choose and use appropriate standard units to estimate and measure length/height in any direction (m/cm) [...] to the nearest appropriate unit, using rulers.

Y2: Statistics: interpret and construct simple tables.

Y2: Geometry: use mathematical vocabulary to describe position, direction and movement, including movement in a straight line [...].

Science

Y1: Plants: identify and describe the basic structure of a variety of common flowering plants.

Y2: Plants: describe how plants need water, light and a suitable temperature to grow.

Y3: Plants: identify and describe the functions of different parts of flowering plants: roots, stem, leaves and flowers.

Y3: Plants: explore the requirements of plants for life and growth (air, light, water [...]).

Background

Plants grow towards the light. It is possible to get plants to grow upwards, sideways and even downwards, by providing light from only one direction.

Plants need sunlight for photosynthesis, which produces the sugars needed for growth and repair. Leaves are usually angled to be able to absorb as much light as possible on their upper surface, which is rich in chloroplasts. Plants in a crowded flower bed or forest often grow at odd angles in order to be able to absorb as much sunlight as possible. Some plants even move during the day, to follow the progress of the sun across the sky; sunflowers do this particularly well. Auxins, plant hormones, are responsible for the bending of the stem towards the light. This activity demonstrates the phototropism (movement towards light) of plants.

Activity

Resources

- Seeds or seedlings: peas, broad beans or sunflowers
- Small pot
- Potting compost
- Small cardboard boxes and tubes
- A strong light or a bright window sill
- Watering can and water
- Cress seedlings

Introduction

Ask the children why a plant needs sunlight to grow. Hopefully some will know about photosynthesis and will understand that without sunlight the plant would 'starve' as it could not make any food. Show the children a dish or picture of germinated cress seeds. Point out how all the little plants grow upwards and ask them to suggest where the light was coming from as the cress grew (Figure 6.7a). Ask what would happen if the cress had been grown in a box with the light coming in from the side. If you have time, set up an experiment with the cress in a box with a hole which only allows light in from the side. Leave it for 24 hours. If there is no time, then show a picture (Figure 6.7b). Discuss how the cress has bent to grow towards the light.

Figure 6.7a Cress grown with light from above

Figure 6.7b Cress grown with light from the side

Show the children a bean, pea or sunflower seedling and ask for their predictions about its behaviour if the light is shining on it from the side.

Main session

The children design their own simple 'maze' to see whether a seedling will grow towards the light. They can use a box or tube to create a light-proof environment and then cut a hole or slit in one side to let light through. It is useful if the box has a removable lid, for watering and inspection. If things go well, then a second box or tube can be added to cause the light to shine from a different direction.

Keep the boxes fairly small so that a result can be seen rapidly. The seedling can be encouraged to grow round a horizontal maze or a more three-dimensional one.

The seedlings need to be planted in suitable compost and watered regularly but not excessively. Time with the lid open should be regulated. Grow a plant in 'normal' light too. Measure the height of the plant grown naturally and the size of its leaves. Compare the measurements to those of the plants in the mazes. Are there differences?

Plenary

How 'clever' was the plant? Did it follow the light? Ask the children how a plant manages to do this; after all, it does not have eyes.

What was the largest angle the seedling could turn through? Could it 'see' light coming from behind it and turn through 180°?

Once the experiment is over, the plant can be allowed to grow in full light. If all goes well, it will flower and produce seeds.

Figure 6.8 A bean in a horizontal maze

Figure 6.9 A sunflower in a vertical maze

Follow-up ideas

Children could consider other factors that determine plant growth. Can they show that gravity has an effect on the direction shoots and roots grow? Can they show how roots grow towards water?

Extension

Challenge the children to show that the pea can grow downwards towards the light. This requires more complex engineering and some thought about the orientation of the pea in space.

Whatever happens, the tip of the seedling always points upwards so there must be another factor involved. Ask the children to think about what else the seedling may be able to sense.

Support

Use a shoe box with holes cut in all four sides and the top. Cover up all but one hole and allow the pea to grow. Once the children have seen which way it is growing, uncover another hole instead.

LIVING WALLS

Objective

- To design a vertical garden, using knowledge of what conditions plants need in order to grow well.

Curriculum links

Mathematics

Y1: **Geometry:** recognise and name common 2-D and 3-D shapes, describe position, direction and movement.
Y3: **Geometry:** identify horizontal and vertical lines and pairs of perpendicular and parallel lines.

Science

Y1: **Plants:** name a variety of common wild and garden plants.
Y2: **Plants:** describe how plants need water, light and a suitable temperature to grow and stay healthy.
Y3: **Plants:** explore the requirements of plants for life and growth and how they vary from plant to plant.

D&T

Design

KS1: design purposeful, functional, appealing products for themselves and other users based on design criteria.
KS2: use research and develop design criteria to inform the design of innovative, functional, appealing products that are fit for purpose [...].

Technical knowledge

KS1: explore and use mechanisms in their products.

KS2: understand and use mechanical systems in their products.

Background

As gardens become smaller, many people are choosing to have a vertical garden. This way they can enjoy a green space without using up all the horizontal surfaces. These living walls have benefits beyond the aesthetic: they can help to insulate buildings and also keep homes cooler in summer as they do not absorb and retain heat from the sun. They provide a habitat for insects and can improve urban air quality. Look for living walls on large, newly built office blocks and shopping centres. The Westfield Shopping Centre in London has one of the UK's longest living walls. There are plenty of commercial planting systems available, but it is also easy to produce a home-made system and recycle some plastics at the same time.

Activity

Resources

- A variety of plants: some with flowers, some with coloured foliage, herbs and trailing species. Check the Royal Horticultural Society's website (www.rhs.org.uk) for lots of helpful information on suitable plants
- Small pots and bottles
- Potting compost
- Watering can and water
- A wall: this could be a wooden fence panel, a pallet, a pinboard or a plank
- Hammer and nails

Introduction

Discuss with the children the conditions that are required for plants to grow well.

Talk about living walls. Where might the children have seen one? Where might a vertical flower bed be better than a horizontal one? What plants might be suitable to grow in such a system? Show the children some pictures of living walls. Discuss why they could be a good way to bring green to city centres.

Discuss the problems of caring for plants in a living wall. The plants may need watering so how will they reach the highest ones? How can the water be prevented from draining instantly down to the ground, flooding the lowest plants and leaving the top ones dry?

Main session

In teams, the children plan their own living wall. If this is to be a feature of the classroom or school, then each team could design one 'column' and then all the columns are combined to produce one collaborative wall.

Children need to consider:

- what containers to use – the size and shape;
- how the containers will be attached to the wall (Figure 6.10);
- what plants to use – size, colour, scent etc.;
- how to water the finished column and how to prevent the water draining straight out again.

Figure 6.10 One way to fix pots to a plank – this method uses metal plant ties that have been formed into a ring and then stapled to the wood

Using plant labels, catalogues or the internet, the children can design the planting in their column, taking into account the needs of the plants. For example, a bushy or trailing plant planted above a plant that needs full sun is not wise.

They should consider how to make the planting structure and perhaps carry out some tests to find out how strong the containers need to be and whether they can be nailed or glued successfully to the wall. They could also design a watering system.

If possible, the children make their living wall.

Plenary

Consider the different designs and solutions to the watering problem. Apart from the planting scheme, which can be individual, it may be better to decide on one structure to be used for the whole wall. If appropriate, the living wall can be assembled, planted and enjoyed! If there is not room for a proper living wall, then the children can make hanging walls: the pots can be suspended one under the other and hung from a hanging basket hook at school or at home.

Figure 6.11 A living wall made from canvas

Figure 6.12 A living wall made from yoghurt pots

Follow-up ideas

Document the success or otherwise of the planting schemes and structural engineering.

If it is not possible to have at school, try to arrange to find a location for the living wall at a child's home or in a local garden. It is so rewarding to see something that has been made with such care admired by others!

Go large! Get the whole school to design and make columns for the wall, then it could be used as an eye-catching addition to the school entrance.

Extension

Children could design a watering system for a living wall that was taller than they could reach. They could use mechanisms such as pulleys to hoist the water up to the top but need to design a way to tip the watering can so that the water flows out.

Children could design a wall with a specific purpose. Herb walls are popular in kitchens, but how about a fruit and vegetable wall or a wall to attract bees or butterflies?

Support

Use a commercial hanging planter bag, which the children can plant with a selection of flowering plants or herbs.

There are several 'how to' guides available on the internet for building a living wall and, although many of them assume use of commercial planting systems, they do provide guidance about suitable plants.

MEET A TREE

Objective

- To learn about trees and to observe them closely.

Curriculum links

Mathematics

Y1: Measurement: compare, describe and solve practical problems for lengths and heights, measure and begin to record lengths and heights.

Y2: Measurement: choose and use appropriate standard units to estimate and measure length/height in any direction (m/cm) […] to the nearest appropriate unit, using rulers.

Y4: Measurement: find the area of a rectilinear shape by counting squares.

Y5: Measurement: calculate and compare the area of rectangles […] and estimate the area of irregular shapes.

Y6: Geometry: illustrate and name parts of circles, including radius, diameter and circumference.

Science

Y1: Plants: identify and name a variety of common wild and garden plants including deciduous and evergreen trees.

Y1: Plants: identify and describe the basic structure of a variety of common flowering plants including trees.

Y2: Plants: observe and describe how seeds grow into mature plants.

Y3: Plants: identify and describe the different parts of flowering plants: roots, stem/trunk, leaves and flowers.

Background

Trees are green plants just like cress, but much bigger! They have the same requirements for growth and reproduction as smaller plants. They can live for a very long time; some of the oldest oak trees in England are more than 800 years old. This is something that fascinates children and makes a great link to history.

Activity

Resources

- 30 m+ measuring tape
- Metre wheel
- Pencils, paper and tape
- Double-sided tape
- Wax crayons
- Calculator
- Tree identification guide (The Woodland Trust does an excellent one)
- Photocopiables: How to estimate the age of a tree (p. 93); How to measure the height of a tree with a pencil (p. 94); How to make a clinometer (p. 95); How to use a clinometer to measure the height of a tree (p. 96)

Introduction

Go for a walk in a woodland area or forest. Look at all the trees and discuss how they are the same and how they are different.

Remind children that trees are green plants and ask them to identify the standard set of parts: stem, leaf, flower and roots.

Main session

Children choose their own tree and 'get to know it':

1 Using a tree identification guide they should decide what type of tree it is. They can use the leaves, bark and seeds to help them with the identification. If there are no seeds visible on the tree, it is worthwhile looking on the ground underneath the tree. If possible, pick one leaf to keep.
2 Make a bark rubbing. One child holds the paper firmly onto the tree trunk while another rubs firmly and thoroughly all over the paper with a wax crayon. Eventually, the pattern of the bark will become apparent.
3 Calculate how old the tree is (see Resources).
4 Measure how tall the tree is (see Resources).

Plenary

Children combine all their data into one information sheet, sticking the leaf and any seeds onto the sheet too (Figure 6.13).

Children could calculate the speed at which the trees have grown by dividing the height by the age of the tree. They could compare this to their own growth rate. If possible, show children a cross section of a tree trunk pointing out the rings showing the yearly growth. Are the rings all the same width?

Figure 6.13 Tree information sheets arranged in order of age

Follow-up ideas

Make a time line showing when the trees started life. Add key historical moments to the time line.
    Investigate whether the tallest trees are always the oldest.
    Calculate the surface area of a leaf. Draw round it on squared paper and count the squares. Estimate the number of leaves on a branch and the number of branches on the tree and so work out the total surface area of all the leaves.

Extension

Beech, hornbeam, lime and hazel trees all have very similar leaves, so ask children to find a way to distinguish between them.
    Measure the height of the tree using a clinometer and simple trigonometry (see Resources).

Support

Choose trees that are easy to identify such as oak or horse chestnut.
    Make sure the tree is not crowded in with a lot of others, which makes identification complex.

GROW A MEAL

Objective

- To grow vegetables and salad in order to make a healthy meal.

Curriculum links

Mathematics

   Y2: Measurement: recognise and use symbols for pounds (£) and pence (p); combine
        amounts to make a particular value, find different combinations of coins that equal
        the same amounts of money, solve simple problems in a practical context involving
        addition and subtraction of money of the same unit, including giving change.
   Y3: Measurement: add and subtract amounts of money to give change, using both £ and
        p in practical contexts.
   Y5: Measurement: use all four operations to solve problems involving […] money using
        decimal notation, including scaling.

Science

   Y1: Plants: identify and name a variety of common wild and garden plants.
   Y2: Plants: find out and describe how plants need water, light and a suitable temperature
        to grow and stay healthy.
   Y2: Animals, including humans: describe the importance for humans of exercise, eating
        the right amounts of different types of food, and hygiene.
   Y3: Plants: explore the requirements of plants for life and growth.
   Y3: Plants: explore the part that flowers play in the life cycle of flowering plants.
   Y3: Animals, including humans: identify that animals, including humans, need the right
        types and amount of nutrition.
   Y4: Animals, including humans: construct and interpret a variety of food chains.

D&T

Cooking and nutrition

KS1: understand where food comes from.

KS2: [...] know where and how a variety of ingredients are grown.

Background

The aim of this activity is that children grow food to eat. This encourages healthy eating and also gives children the opportunity to try out vegetables that they may not have eaten before. It is far more interesting to eat home-grown produce than to eat something bought from a supermarket.

It takes a long time to grow some vegetables from seed so it is worthwhile considering how to organise this activity. It may be that you want to start when the seeds have germinated and grown to a suitable-sized plant, or you may want the children to start with seeds and follow the process through. If starting with ready-germinated seedlings, ask around for help to produce enough seedlings for all the children. Enthusiastic gardeners and allotment holders may be happy to propagate the seeds in advance. Most food plants can also be bought as plugs from garden centres.

Activity

Resources

- Seeds/small plants: cress, radish, sweetcorn, tomato, carrot, pea, bean, lettuce, courgette
- Optional: Seed potatoes, strawberry plants
- Garden plot or large containers
- Suitable potting compost
- Small pots or seed trays
- Watering can and water

Introduction

Show the children examples of vegetables and salad. Discuss which ones the children have tried and which they like. Ask if anyone eats home-grown vegetables or whether they buy everything in a shop. Explain how easy it is to grow food plants; just plant the seed, give it the right conditions and the plant will do the rest!

Explain the challenge to the children: they are going to grow a meal. They can decide what to grow, but everything must be ready to eat at the same time.

Show seed packets, or plant information, which will allow children to find out how long they can expect to have to wait until they have a vegetable ready to eat. Remind them that they should plan when to plant each type of seed so that everything is ready at the same time.

Main session

Children choose what to plant. If there is limited space, this can be a whole-class project, with everyone working to care for the same vegetable plot on a rota. If there is more space available, then the children could be divided into smaller teams, each with their own plot. The children should plan what to plant where in their plots. If space is limited, then nearly all vegetables can be grown successfully in pots (Figure 6.14).

The children can monitor the growth and development of the plants over time. Eventually, the vegetables and fruit can be harvested and eaten.

Figure 6.14 Vegetable plants growing successfully in a plastic washing-up bowl

Plenary

Did anyone successfully plan, grow and harvest a meal? Did any plants grow more slowly, or faster than expected? What problems did the children encounter when growing the plants?

Organise a taste test. Do home-grown vegetables taste better than the ones from the supermarket?

Show the children the price of the seeds, or seedlings. They can work out how much their vegetables cost and compare that to the price of shop-bought vegetables. Discuss why there is a difference in price.

Follow-up ideas

Children can plan and make salads, sandwiches and soups from the vegetables.

Go large! Start growing vegetables on a much bigger scale. Could they be used for school dinners or for D&T food technology? Many schools already grow their own vegetables and there is a wealth of information and support available.

Extension

Give children a budget for their market garden. They must buy the seeds, plants and compost. They might also purchase help with planting out and watering. Once grown, the children could calculate a price to sell their produce in order to earn back the cost of production (or even make a profit).

Challenge children to grow vegetables that take different lengths of time to reach maturity. Can they plan ahead and work out when they should plant each seed? Give them a blank calendar to help.

Support

Choose quick-growing seeds such as cress and radish and use ready-grown plants such as tomato and strawberry.

Grow plants in advance so that the produce can be harvested within a few weeks of planting out. This involves considerable forward planning.

PLANTS FOR BUILDING

Objective

- To consider the properties of various plants that make them useful building materials.

Curriculum links

Mathematics

Y2: Measurement: choose and use appropriate standard units to estimate and measure length/height in any direction (m/cm), mass (kg/g); […] to the nearest appropriate unit, using rulers, scales.
Y2: Statistics: interpret and construct simple tables.
Y5: Geometry: know angles are measured in degrees: estimate and compare acute, obtuse and reflex angles, draw given angles, and measure them in degrees (°).

Science

Y1: Everyday materials: describe the simple physical properties of a variety of everyday materials.
Y2: Uses of everyday materials: compare the suitability of a variety of everyday materials for particular uses.
Y5: Properties and changes of materials: give reasons based on evidence from comparative and fair tests for the particular use of everyday materials.

D&T

Technical knowledge

KS1: build structures, exploring how they can be made stronger, stiffer and more stable.
KS2: apply their understanding of how to strengthen, stiffen and reinforce more complex structures.

Background

Natural materials have always been used for building. Plants offer strength, flexibility and hardness and can be shaped either naturally or using tools. This activity challenges the children to use only natural materials to build a structure.

Activity

Resources

- Bamboo canes
- Cotton: fabric and thread
- Ivy
- Reeds, straw or raffia
- Twigs, particularly from willow and silver birch
- Jute string
- Turf (optional)

Introduction

Explain that the children are going to try to build a model house using only natural materials. Show them the materials available and discuss where they come from.

Ask the children to think about the properties of the materials needed to build a structure. Some should be rigid, but others might need to be flexible. Does anything need to be waterproof?

Main session

The children test the various materials to discover their properties:

1 Strength: hang weights carefully from each material. Keep adding more until the material breaks.
2 Flexibility: measure how much the material can bend before it snaps. Goggles and thick gloves should be used, or this can be done as a demonstration. Use a large protractor or circle marked in 10° units to give a measure of the angle of bend.
3 Mass: weigh similar-sized samples of each material.

Children can then prepare an information sheet about the materials they have tested. Using the information, they can decide what material is suitable for what role in the building of a structure. Once planned, if there is sufficient material, the children can build their structure. You may want to have a design brief for this: height, floor area inside, addition of an entrance door and windows, waterproof etc.

In order to help the structures stay stable, the children could build on turf. Sticks can be pushed into the turf to stand upright. The hut in Figure 6.15 was assembled on a square of turf in a tray. The hut was strong and stable even as the turf dried out.

Figure 6.15 A hut made from woven silver-birch twigs with a raffia thatch

Plenary

Test the structures against the criteria in the design brief.

Discuss why the children chose to use a particular material for a particular role.

Follow-up ideas

Once the structures have been evaluated and enjoyed, they can be filled with small twigs, bamboo, pine cones or dead leaves and placed outside to become minibeast hotels.

Go large! Make a building that at least two children can fit inside, using only natural materials.

Research homes around the world and see how natural materials are used in other countries. Look at new low environmental-impact buildings and identify what they are made from. Are the materials all natural?

Extension

Extend the design brief to include more structural elements: ask that the structure can support a load, or that it can withstand a strong sideways force from the wind.

Limit the materials available so that children have to think of the best possible way to utilise the resources.

Support

Use a smaller selection of materials: bamboo, jute string and a square of cotton fabric can be made into a super shelter.

SUNFLOWER RACE

Objective

- To observe how high and how fast sunflower plants can grow.

Curriculum links

Mathematics

Y2: Measurement: choose and use appropriate standard units to estimate and measure length/height in any direction (m/cm) [...] to the nearest appropriate unit, using rulers.
Y2: Statistics: interpret and construct simple tables, ask and answer questions about totalling and comparing categorical data.
Y3: Measurement: measure, compare, add and subtract: lengths (m/cm/mm), compare durations of events [for example, to calculate the time taken by particular events or tasks].
Y4: Statistics: interpret and present discrete and continuous data using appropriate graphical methods, including bar charts and time graphs, solve comparison, sum and difference problems using information presented in [...] tables and other graphs.
Y5: Measurement: use all four operations to solve problems involving measure [...] using decimal notation, including scaling.

Science

Y1: Plants: identify and describe the basic structure of a variety of common flowing plants.
Y2: Plants: observe and describe how seeds grow into mature plants.
Y2: Plants: find out and describe how plants need water, light and a suitable temperature to grow and stay healthy.
Y3: Plants: explore the requirements of plants for life and growth.

D&T

Technical knowledge

KS1: build structures, exploring how they can be made stronger, stiffer and more stable.
KS2: apply their understanding of how to strengthen, stiffen and reinforce more complex structures.

Background

Sunflowers grow tall, but can the conditions they are grown in affect how fast and how high they grow? Using their knowledge of green plants, the children can give their sunflower the best possible chance to win the race. As the sunflowers grow, the children can investigate the structure of stems by building their own, life-size sunflower from paper straws.

Activity

Resources

- Sunflower seeds
- Plant pots
- Potting compost or soil
- Watering can and water
- Metre sticks or measuring tapes
- Space in a flower bed, if possible
- Paper straws
- Paper leaf shapes of various sizes
- Tape or glue
- Scissors

Introduction

Explain the challenge: to grow the tallest sunflower in the fastest possible time.

Children can decide what factors affect growth and height. They may decide that enough water and plenty of sunlight will be best. They might try growing the sunflowers in very large pots. They might think about the importance of the type of compost used.

Main session

Children decide on the conditions for their sunflower, set up the pot and plant their seeds.

Germination occurs after about one week. Once the plants have emerged, their height can be measured and recorded regularly. Graphs can be plotted by hand or using a graph-plotting program to show how the plants are growing.

Figure 6.16 Life-size model sunflowers. Note: the stem of the tallest sunflower proved too weak to hold up the plant even though it was three times as thick as the other models.

Children can also record the number and pattern of the leaves that grow. They could try to measure or estimate the area of the leaves.

Growing sunflowers in pots will limit their growth and it is best, once the children have spent four or five weeks measuring, if the plants are transferred to a flower bed to continue to grow.

Once the sunflower has flowered, the competition comes to an end.

At various points over the weeks of growth, challenge the children to build their own, life-size sunflower, using paper straws. They will see that the sunflower is self-supporting, so their models must be too. Provide leaf shapes that the children can add to the stem in the correct pattern. As more leaves are added, the stem will need to be made stronger. This might mean that they use several straws taped together to make a rigid-enough stem.

Discuss how the plants manage to stay self-supporting. If possible, stop watering one plant and watch as it wilts.

Plenary

Which sunflower grew tallest? Was the tallest sunflower also the one that grew fastest?

Once the results are in, ask the children to decide whether the conditions they chose made a difference to the growth of the sunflower. Sometimes, even in identical conditions, sunflowers will grow to different heights. This is probably a genetic effect. Set up a few sunflowers in 'poor' conditions so that children can compare growth with their own plant.

Discuss the number and sizes of the leaves produced and why the plants need such large leaves.

Follow-up ideas

Use the seeds from the flower heads to grow more plants, or use them as bird food.

Compare sunflower growth to human growth. Measure the children over the same time interval and see whether they change in size. The arrangement of the seeds in the flower head can be linked to the Fibonacci activity in Chapter 4.

Extension

Ask the children to calculate the speed of growth using the data and the equation:

speed = change in height ÷ time taken

It is possible to weigh the flower heads using a spring balance or force meter. Challenge the children to make their model sunflower capable of supporting the same mass of flower head as the real sunflower.

Support

Put a bamboo cane beside the plant and stick on a marker each day to show how the plant has grown. This provides a visual record of growth without the need for a graph. The children can see how the plant's height changes each day and also can see how the speed of growth changes by looking at the spaces between the markers.

Create the life-size sunflowers by gluing the straws to cardboard so that they do not 'wilt' when leaves are added. Focus on the size and the pattern of leaves rather than on the structural integrity of the models.

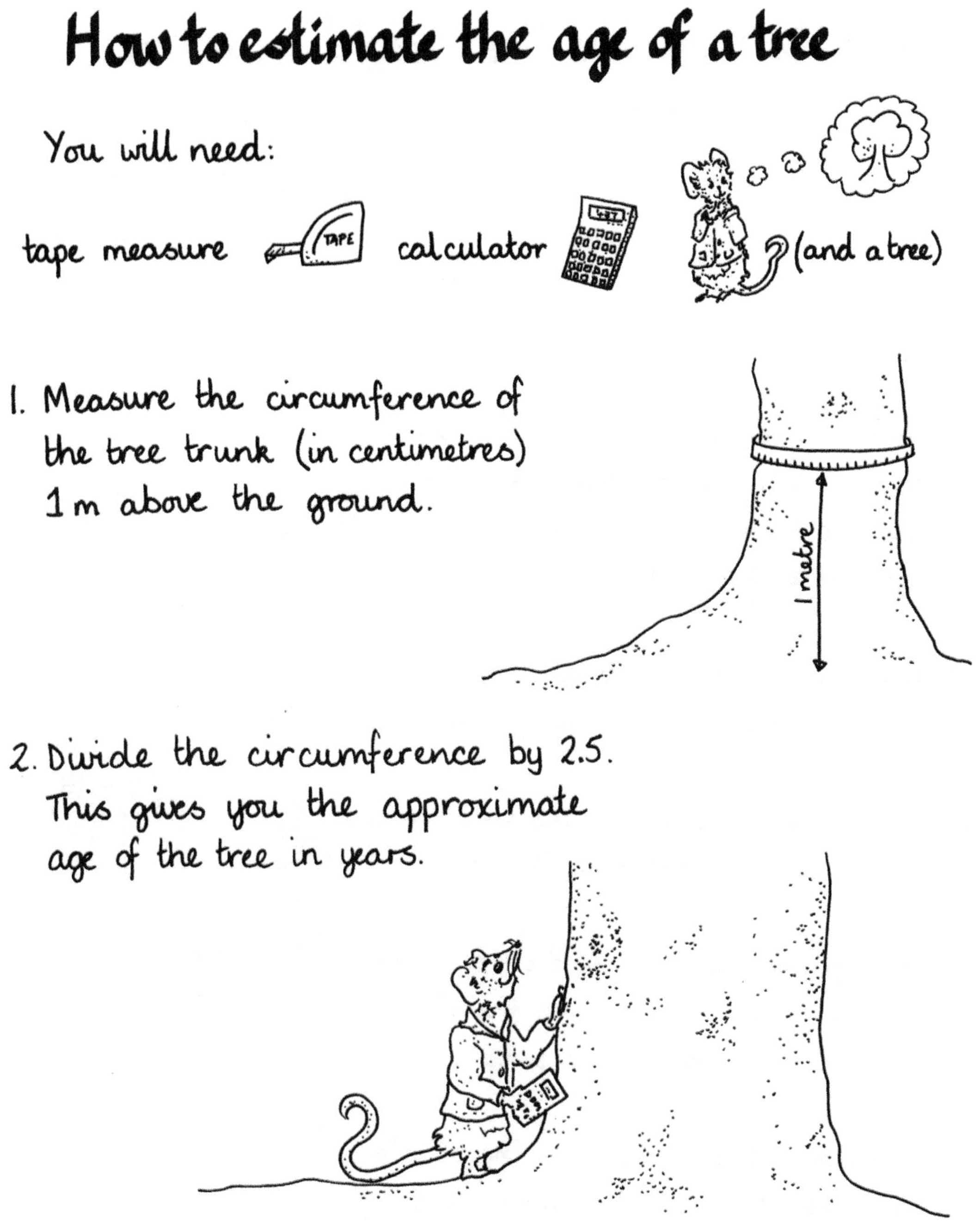
How to estimate the age of a tree
You will need:
tape measure
TAPE
calculator
(and a tree)
1. Measure the circumference of the tree trunk (in centimetres) 1 m above the ground.
1 metre
2. Divide the circumference by 2.5. This gives you the approximate age of the tree in years.

Figure 6.17

How to measure the height of a tree with a pencil

You will need:

pencil ✏️   tape measure 📏   friend 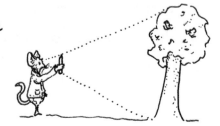 (and a tree)

1. Hold pencil upright in front of you at arm's length.

2. Walk backwards until the top of the pencil is level with the top of the tree and the bottom of the pencil is level with the bottom of the tree.

3. Carefully, tip the pencil sideways until it is horizontal, still holding it at arm's length.

4. Make sure the bottom of the pencil is still in line with the bottom of the tree.

5. Ask a friend to stand by the tree, then to walk away until you see them in line with the other end of the pencil.

6. Measure the distance from the tree to your friend. This is the same as the height of the tree.

Figure 6.18

How to make a clinometer

You will need:

thick card   string   tube (wide straw or pen barrel)

pen

protractor   weight   scissors

tape

1. Cut a quarter circle from the card.

2. Make a notch in one of the straight edges, 1 cm in from the right angled corner.

3. Draw a straight line from the notch to the curved edge, parallel to the other straight edge. This is your 0° line.

4. Using a protractor, mark angles from 0° to 90°, around the point of the notch.

5. Tape the tube to the notched edge.

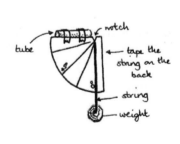

6. Hang the string over the notch, with most hanging down the front. Tape the string to the back of the clinometer. Tie a weight to the string.

7. Look through the tube. The weight will swing as you tilt the clinometer.

Figure 6.19

How to use a clinometer to measure the height of a tree

You will need:

your clinometer   tape measure    (and a tree)

1. Check that 45° is marked on your clinometer.

2. Hold the tube to your eye and look through it at the top of the tree.

3. Move backwards or forwards until the string hangs along the 45° mark when you can see the top of the tree through the tube.

4. Measure the distance from the tree to where you are standing. This is x.

5. Measure the distance from the ground to your eye (y).

          x + y = height of tree

6. Add together x and y (your distance from the tree and the distance of your eye from the ground).

Figure 6.20

CHAPTER 7

Help!

7.1 Heliographs

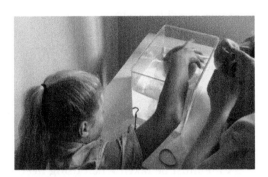

7.2 Buoyancy aids

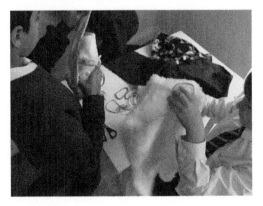

7.3 Wind chill

7.4 Whistles

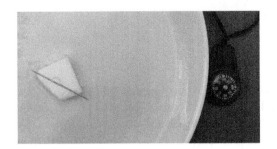

7.5 Compasses

7.6 Beachcombing

OVERVIEW

The activities in this chapter are linked by a survival theme. Staying alive and communicating are two important factors if one wishes to survive a shipwreck or becoming lost in the wilderness. These activities are not designed to be a training course for survival but rather to look at the STEM factors behind survival.

HEALTH AND SAFETY

Remind the children that they should never look directly at the Sun and that no light rays, whether from sun or torch, should be directed into another person's eyes. Make targets from paper for the children to 'hit' instead.

Take care with water; ensure that splashes are mopped up and that no electrical equipment is close enough to become wet. Water at 50°C should be safe to touch, but exercise caution nevertheless.

One hundred gram masses are heavy. It may be safer for children to work on the floor so that dropped masses have a less damaging effect.

Ensure that fan blades cannot be touched by small fingers. Check that nothing can be blown over by the strong air flow from the fan.

Avoid using very loud, very high notes as these could damage the ear.

Care must be taken when using needles. Push the points into cork or rubber to prevent injury.

HELIOGRAPHS

Objective

- To investigate the reflective properties of mirrors.
- To use a protractor to accurately reflect light rays in a chosen direction.

Curriculum links

Mathematics

Y5: Geometry: know angles are measured in degrees: estimate and compare acute, obtuse and reflex angles, draw given angles and measure them in degrees (°).

Science

Y2: Uses of everyday materials: identify and compare the suitability of everyday materials […] for particular uses.
Y3: Light: notice that light is reflected from surfaces.
Y6: Light: recognise that light appears to travel in straight lines.

Background

A heliograph is a signalling device that works by reflecting sunlight from a movable mirror. It can be used to send messages in Morse code because the beam of reflected light can be interrupted by covering the mirror. It was used in the late 19th and early 20th centuries by survey teams and by the military. In fact, heliographs were standard issue in the British army until the 1960s. Many survival kits still contain a mirror or are packed in a shiny tin, which can be used as a reflector. Depending on the size of the mirror and the clarity of the view, heliograph signals can be seen up to 30 miles (48 km) away. Unless one is standing in the direct path of the beam, it is almost impossible to see, so it was a relatively secure form of communication. The disadvantages are obvious: it will not work on a cloudy day or at night.

Resources

- Mirrors: flat, concave and convex
- A protractor
- Torch or other light source
- Large sheets of black and white paper
- A playing field or park with wide views

Introduction

Show the children some pictures of heliographs and explain how they were used. Darken the classroom and, using a mirror and light from a torch, show how it is possible to reflect the torch beam around the room. Use your hand or a piece of card to cover the mirror and flash out SOS in Morse code.

Ask the children to try to explain what is happening to the light and how the mirror helps to move the beam around. The children should talk about 'reflecting' in their explanations.

Explain how, before electricity and wireless communications became common, the heliograph provided a useful long-distance communication system.

Main session

The children can investigate reflection using a flat mirror and a torch. By shining the torch at a mirror, the children can follow the light beam from the torch and the reflected beam from the mirror. They should see that a pattern emerges. As they change the angle of the torch beam, the reflected ray changes direction too. The angles the beam and the reflected ray make with the mirror should be the same. This can be checked using a protractor.

Figure 7.7 Using a torch and mirror to investigate reflection – the torch light can be made into a clear beam by shining it through a piece of card with a slot cut in it

Children can use this knowledge to reflect the torch beam to particular points in the room. Tape the torch to the table and ask the children to move mirrors around until the beam lands on large pieces of paper fastened to the table, wall or ceiling.

For older children: once the children are confident about using a mirror to reflect a beam of light where they want, discuss how the heliograph uses the Sun as a light source. The Sun is usually high in the sky so hang a torch above a flipchart or white board and draw the light beam as it shines down. Then draw the required route of the reflected ray. Ask the children to work out how to reflect the light in this direction. Using a mirror, the children can adjust the angle until the beam hits the mirror and is reflected in the correct direction (Figure 7.8).

Go outside and using the mirror, ask the children to send the sunlight to various points on the field. If possible, send a group of children as far away as possible and then signal to them using the mirror.

Plenary

Discuss the success of heliographs as a signalling method. Ask the children to think about the problems soldiers and castaways might have when wanting to signal using a mirror.

Ask the children to use several large mirrors to direct a light beam around the room and back to where it started, or to direct the beam out of a door and down a corridor. If the children have understood the principle of reflection, they should be able to do this without too much problem.

Figure 7.8 Student teachers working out where to place the mirror in order to direct the Sun's rays to hit one of the points marked on the flip chart

Follow-up ideas

Go large! How far can you send a message with your mirror heliograph? Could you send a message from one headland to another at the seaside?

Are flat mirrors best? Investigate what happens with curved mirrors.

Extension

The Sun changes position in the sky during the day so ask the children to think about the angles required to hit the same spot early in the morning, at midday and late afternoon. Is it possible to send messages to and from the same places all day or will the Sun's position in the sky make that impossible?

Ask the children to direct a light beam to a point behind the torch. They may need to use two or more mirrors.

Support

Figure 7.9 Using two mirrors to turn a torch beam through 180°

Use large mirrors and strong torches so that the reflected ray is easy to spot. Keep distances shorter while the children investigate.

Draw lines on a paper at 30°, 45°, 70° and 90° to the mirror to show how to direct the torch towards the mirror. The children can draw on the line of the reflected ray and can measure the angle using a simplified protractor with the same angles (30°, 45°, 70°, 90°) marked on it.

BUOYANCY AIDS

Objective

- To investigate buoyancy.
- To calculate volumes of unusual shapes using formulae including pi and other methods.

Curriculum links

Mathematics

> **Y5: Measurement:** use all four operations to solve problems involving measure [...] using decimal notation, including scaling.
>
> **Y6: Measurement:** solve problems involving the calculation and conversion of units of measure, using decimal notation up to three decimal places where appropriate.

Science

> **Y5: Forces:** No direct links but extends learning.

Background

Buoyancy aids or life jackets should always be available on journeys that involve transport over, on or in water. These add volume but not mass to our bodies, decreasing our density and helping us to float rather than sink. Therefore, most flotation devices are large but light. Density is calculated as: density = mass ÷ volume. As the volume of an object increases, its density decreases. This can be demonstrated using a balloon. Pour water into a balloon until it sinks. Then, with the water still inside it, blow up the balloon to increase its volume. It will float on water.

Anything that can be filled with air can help someone to float, so shipwrecked sailors may hang on to an empty barrel or even an air-filled plastic bag to help them float to safety. The old ASA Personal Survival courses used to include making a float from pyjama trousers.

Resources

- Inflatable arm bands
- Balloons
- A stone
- 50 g or 100 g masses
- String or elastic bands
- Ruler
- Tank of water
- Photocopiable: How to calculate the volume of a balloon (p. 112)

Introduction

Show the children the arm bands and ask them what effect they have on a person in the water.

Show the children an uninflated balloon and a stone (weighing about 100 g) and ask them how they could stop the stone sinking in water. Someone may suggest blowing up the balloon to use it like an arm band or life jacket. Demonstrate.

Main session

The children investigate how the volume of a balloon is linked to the weight of object it can support.

Children inflate the balloons to different sizes and record how many 50 g or 100 g masses each balloon can support. They can record the total mass supported or convert the mass into Newtons and record the weight supported (100 g = 1 N). The masses can be attached to the balloon with string or elastic bands (Figure 7.10)

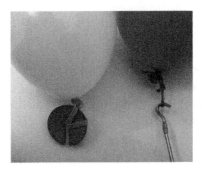

Figure 7.10 Masses attached to balloons using string or elastic bands

In order to work out the volume of the balloons, the children can:

1   Inflate the balloons using a pump and count the number of pumps used.
2   Inflate the balloons and then get a rough estimate of volume by pushing the balloon gently into a series of containers of known volume (ice-cream tubs and measuring cups work well).
3   Assume the balloon is a sphere or a cylinder and use the appropriate equations (see Resources).

Plenary

Ask the children to describe and explain the patterns they observed.

Set the children some challenges using heavy objects. Can they work out what size balloon will be needed to support the object? Some objects may need the help of more than one balloon. Once they have decided on the volume of balloon required, they can test their predictions.

Discuss why life jackets can save lives and how floating helps people to stay alive in the water.

Follow-up ideas

Use different shaped balloons. Using the counted pumps method (method 1 above), fill different shaped balloons with the same amount of air and see whether they are able to support the same weight.

If you can get hold of old, unwanted buoyancy aids, the children could look at how they are made and investigate the properties of the floatation materials.

Ask a member of the RNLI to visit to talk to the children about water safety.

Extension

Add lots of salt to the water and repeat the experiment. What do the children notice?

Water provides an upwards force called upthrust, which means that an object weighing 100 g (1 N) in air will weigh less in water (about 0.8 N). Children can weigh in water by hanging objects from a force meter and submerging the object (but not the force meter!). They can record the weight of each object in water in N and calculate the actual weight each balloon supports.

Support

Use counted pumps (method 1) and inflate balloons with one, two, four and eight pumps so that the volumes are related (doubled or halved) and can be compared.

WIND CHILL

Objective

- To investigate the insulating properties of various fabrics.
- To read and plot temperature data using a thermometer or temperature probe.
- To demonstrate how evaporation from a warm body leads to cooling.

Curriculum links

Mathematics

Y2: Measurement: choose and use appropriate standard units to estimate and measure […] temperature (°C) to the nearest appropriate unit using […] thermometers.
Y2: Statistics: interpret and construct […] simple tables.
Y4: Statistics: interpret and present discrete and continuous data using appropriate graphical methods, including bar charts and time graphs.
Y5 Statistics: solve comparison, sum and difference problems using information presented in a line graph.

Science

Y2: Uses of everyday materials: identify and compare the suitability of everyday materials […] for particular uses.
Y5: Properties and changes of materials: give reasons based on evidence from comparative or fair tests for the particular uses of everyday materials […].

D&T

Make

KS1: select from and use a wide range of materials […] including textiles […] according to their characteristics.
KS2: select from and use a wider range of materials […] including textiles […] according to their functional properties and aesthetic qualities.

Background

Wind chill is a very real danger on cold days. The air close to the body, which has been warmed by body heat, can be 'blown away' and replaced by colder air, chilling the body sometimes to dangerous levels. Calculating wind chill is complex, but many weather-forecasting apps will provide wind chill or 'feels like' data, which give some idea of the power of the wind even on a hot day.

If a human body becomes chilled below 35°C then hypothermia sets in. This can be deadly if not treated rapidly and is something that children should be aware of. Elderly people and those who cannot move easily are more prone to chilling than those who move around constantly.

Resources

- Containers with lids e.g. water bottles
- Hot water of about 50°C
- Thermometers or dataloggers with temperature probes
- Selection of different fabrics

- Elastic bands or tape
- Plastic bags
- Table fan
- Spray bottle

Introduction

Children should already know that they are warmer when they have thick clothes on. They should have some ideas of the clothes they wear to keep warm and what they are made from. Ask for clothing suggestions for various weather conditions such as rainy, sunny, snowy or windy, and ask them to give reasons for their choices.

Introduce the term: wind chill. Depending on the age of the children, some may already know about this. Explain that on a windy day, humans can feel colder than they would at the same temperature on a still day. For example, it often seems hotter in the summer if there is no breeze. Explain why explorers, castaways or survivors from shipwrecks may be affected by wind chill. Ask the children what they should do to protect themselves.

If appropriate, you may consider discussing the dangers of hypothermia.

Main session

Children investigate body cooling. Using containers filled with water at about 50°C, they plot the temperature decrease over time. The children should compare a 'naked' body and one that has a suitable fabric securely wrapped around it. They should notice a difference in the rate of cooling of the body. Using a thermometer placed in the water, they can record 'body temperature' every five minutes. The temperatures can be plotted on a graph. Cooling is quite slow at these temperatures. An uninsulated bottle of water at 50°C takes about 45 minutes to cool to below 37°C.

Now add in wind chill. Repeat the experiment but with the containers placed in front of a fan turning as fast as possible. Temperatures can be measured and plotted again.

Figure 7.11 Measuring wind chill – the small strips of cloth show that there is a breeze blowing

Plenary

Discuss the results. What happens to the temperature of a 'naked' body in the wind? What was the effect of the clothing?

Were some fabrics better than others at keeping the body warm? Introduce or reinforce the word: insulation. Look at the structures of the fabrics that kept the water warmest. What do they have in common? If the children all investigate different fabrics then the best fabric(s) can be used to design a survival suit. This may be made from several layers of different fabrics. It can then be tested.

There are many different ways to combine and compare the data collected from these experiments. This is a good opportunity to show the power of graphs!

Follow-up ideas

Repeat the whole experiment but make the containers and coverings wet. To keep the 'naked' container wet, it will have to have water sprayed on it regularly.

The children could test various technical fabrics that are used for mountaineering/exploring gear. These are normally made from a selection of materials including a water-proof layer, an insulating layer and a soft inner layer. The children can decide the role and importance of each different fabric.

The children could research how polar animals keep warm.

Extension

Cold-weather gear is both insulated and waterproof. Children could investigate the effect of wearing a cagoule by putting a plastic bag over the bottles. How does the plastic bag manage to keep things warmer? They will have to look at the structure of the materials.

Children could calculate the speed of cooling (speed = change in temperature ÷ time).

Support

Using a datalogger and temperature probe connected to a graph plotter will show a real-time cooling curve without the problems of having to read a thermometer and plot a graph.

Use hotter water (with care) as this cools more rapidly and provides a quicker demonstration.

WHISTLES

Objective

- To measure volume in decibels using a sound meter.

Curriculum links

Mathematics

Y4: **Statistics:** interpret and present discrete and continuous data using appropriate graphical methods, including bar charts and time graphs.

Y5: **Statistics:** solve comparison, sum and difference problems using information presented in a line graph.

Y6: **Statistics:** interpret and construct pie charts and line graphs and use these to solve problems.

Science

Y4: **Sound:** find patterns between the pitch of sound and features of the object that produced it.

Y4: **Sound:** recognise that sounds get fainter as the distance from the sound increases.

Background

Most survival packs include a whistle, for attracting attention. Humans hear across a fairly small range of pitch and the mechanics of the human ear mean that it is more sensitive to high-pitched sounds than low-pitched sounds. So, in an emergency, the higher you scream, the more hope you have of being heard and rescued. Whistles are useful for attracting attention because they produce a high-pitched sound (think of a referee's whistle at a football match, which can be heard clearly above all the cheering and singing). Sound is measured in decibels (dB), but most sound meters have been calibrated to human hearing in units called dBA.

Resources

- A sound meter either from a datalogger or as an app (there are free sound-meter apps available)
- A recorder or a recording of high- and low-pitched sounds
- A selection of noise makers: a recorder, a drum, a tambourine, a whistle etc.
- Photocopiable: How to make a straw squeaker (p. 113)

Introduction

Show the children a selection of noise makers. Some should make low-pitched sounds and some high-pitched sounds. Ask the children which will be best for attracting the attention of someone some distance away. Discuss what properties the noise might need to have in order to be clearly heard over some distance.

Explain that volume is a measure of how loud a noise is and that it is measured in decibels. Show how to measure volume using the datalogger or sound-meter app.

Main session

This is best done as a whole-class/group activity with an adult producing the sounds. Using recorders or other suitable instruments, measure the volume of high- and low-pitched notes, using a dBA scale. Try to keep the volume of the notes the same by blowing the recorder with the same force each time. Ask some children to listen and record which note they thought was the loudest and others to record the dBA from a sound meter. The children should also record whether the note was high or low. Repeat the test several times.

It may be easier to have some pre-recorded sounds for the children to measure. Make sure you have a range of pitches from very high to very low. If possible, borrow a sopranino (higher) or tenor (lower) recorder to increase the range of notes available to test.

With luck, the children's results will show that high-pitched noises are louder on the dBA scale

Plenary

Record the children's data in a table. Discuss how the readings vary and why this is happening (different blowing forces, different instruments, the problem getting a steady reading from a sound meter, background noise). Do the measured data correlate with the children's own opinions of the loudness?

Return to the noise makers used in the introduction and ask children again to decide which will be best for attracting attention. Ask them to explain their choice.

Show the children how to make a straw squeaker (see Resources) and let them investigate how length of the straw determines the pitch.

Follow-up ideas

Design and produce an emergency straw whistle, explaining why it should be very short.

The children could measure how far the sound of the recorder travels across a playing field or park. They could test both high- and low-pitched sounds. Again, it is important that the recorder is blown with the same force for all notes.

Children could measure how far the sound of a referee's whistle can travel. They could compare it to the sound of a whistle found on a life jacket.

Extension

The children could investigate a range of instruments made from different materials. For example, they could test a plastic and a wooden recorder and see whether there is a difference in the volume of the same note, played with the same force on the two different recorders.

Support

The children could make their own judgements about how loud the note was, using a numerical scale or a description of the note; this may be about the volume or about the discomfort of the note: high notes are often uncomfortable to hear.

If children are unable to hear, then it is possible to convert sound to an image using an oscilloscope (or suitable app). The oscilloscope trace gives a picture of the pitch of the note so the children can relate the picture to the sound-meter reading. As the sound meter measures in dBA, it is mimicking human hearing, so it is not essential that the children can hear the note in order to participate.

COMPASSES

Objective

- To make a compass by magnetising a steel pin or needle.
- To learn the points of a compass.

Curriculum links

Mathematics

Geometry: No direct links but extends learning.

Science

Y2: Uses of everyday materials: identify and compare the suitability of a variety of everyday materials […] for particular uses.
Y3: Forces and magnets: observe how magnets attract and repel each other […].
Y3: Forces and magnets: describe magnets as having two poles.

Background

The needle of a compass is a magnet. It points North because it aligns itself with the large magnetic field of the Earth. Iron and steel are magnetic metals. This means that they are attracted by a magnet but they can also be magnetised and turned into magnets themselves. To turn a lump of iron or steel into a magnet requires the use of another magnet or an electric current. A magnet can be demagnetised by dropping it onto a hard surface several times. You may have noticed that old magnets are often rather weak and this can be due to a lifetime of careless handling.

Resources

- Steel pins or needles
- A bar magnet
- Polystyrene
- Saucer or glass dish (avoid plastic dishes)
- Water
- Compass
- Photocopiable: How to turn a needle into a compass (p. 114)

Introduction

Ask the children where North is. How could they check their answers?

Show the children a compass and explain how it works. Demonstrate how they could use a compass to help them navigate when using a map.

Main session

Using a magnet and stroking one pole carefully along the length of a needle several times, the children magnetise their needles (see Resources).

Once magnetised, the needle can be placed on a small piece of polystyrene, floating on water, and it should align itself North–South. The children should record which end of their needle points to the North. If the needle does not align itself North–South then more passes with the magnet are required. Children could count how many times they stroke their needle before it becomes a magnet.

The children can draw a compass rose, with the compass points marked on it to use with their needle compass.

Keep some strong magnets handy for retrieving dropped needles and pins.

Plenary

Ask the children to use their needle compasses to work out the compass directions of various objects or buildings around them. They can compare their readings with a 'real' compass.

Using a magnet, show the children what happens to a compass needle if it is too close to another magnet (it swings to align itself with that magnet) and ask them to think about precautions they should take when using a compass. They could check electronic devices for hidden magnets.

Follow-up ideas

Go orienteering with the needle compasses. The children can follow instructions consisting of a compass point and a distance, in steps or in metres to find treasure or clues to a puzzle.

Make a 'proper' compass by designing and making a container in which to hang or float the needle. The container should also incorporate a compass rose.

Extension

Include 8 or 16 compass points on the compass rose.

Using compasses, the children could learn how to divide up a circle into equal-sized segments, to help them to draw an accurate compass rose.

Support

Start with the four major compass points (N, S, E and W) and only add the next four (NW, NE, SW, SE) if the children are confident.

Push the point of the needle into a piece of cork or rubber so that it is safer to hold.

BEACHCOMBING

Objective

- To use a limited set of materials to solve a problem.

Curriculum links

This session covers many curriculum areas; see each individual activity and curriculum map for more details.

Background

This is a very open-ended activity session and can be adjusted to support many different parts of the curriculum. So much junk and waste is washed up onto beaches these days that a diligent beachcomber could probably find all the components he or she needed to build anything at all. In this activity, the children are provided with a collection of junk materials and a problem. They use the junk to produce an article that will solve the problem. Some examples are given below but the scope is limited only by time and imagination!

This is also a good opportunity to address the problems of pollution in the oceans.

Resources

- Junk materials: card, plastic, wood, fabric
- String, glue, staples, nails, tape as appropriate
- Specialist 'junk' specific to the task: see activity guide
- Scissors, saws, hammers etc., according to need

Introduction

Explain the scenario: the children are castaways on a desert island, or lost in a jungle or on a mountain. As luck would have it, they have come across some washed-up crates or a rusting container full of useful items. They can use this and the various tools available, to solve the problem. To save space, most solutions will have to be small-scale models rather than life size.

Main session

Children investigate the materials they have been provided with and design a way to solve the problem.

Make a torch or signalling light

In the crate are wires, bulbs, some batteries and bits of metal and foil. Children should try to build a circuit to light a bulb and also make a switch to be able to turn the lights on and off. Extension challenge (hard!): make a light for a landing strip for a rescue plane. Children can also think about how they might mark out the landing strip (perhaps with white stones or white plastic bottles) (*Y4 and Y6 Electricity*).

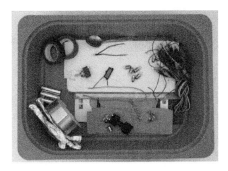

Figure 7.12a Electricity beachcombing crate

Figure 7.12b A torch and a landing strip (made with adult help)

Find out what is in the unlabelled cans

The crate contains a lot of food cans but most of them have lost their labels. Thankfully, one example of each still has a label on. The children have to think of ways to identify what is in the other cans without opening them. Use cans containing different types of food e.g. a runny soup, dog/cat food, meatballs in sauce, baked beans, fruit. The cans may look different; they may have dates or numbers printed on them; they may weigh different amounts; they will behave differently if rolled down a slope (cans containing runny soups do not roll as far as cans containing thicker liquids). The children can devise ways to test the cans (*Y2 Measurement*).

Figure 7.13 Testing the unlabelled cans by rolling them down a shallow slope

Build an escape float

Use the junk to build a raft. The junk should include lots of plastic bottles, wood and string or wire (*Y1, Y2 Everyday materials*).

Figure 7.14a Escape float crate

Figure 7.14b Completed escape float

Build furniture for the camp

Provide wood, bamboo canes, strong fabric such as canvas, string and some small nails or drawing pins. The children can try to make a chair, table, shelves or bed. Once again, this could be model size or scaled up to child size depending on resources. Do not provide glue or tape but encourage the children to lash the wood together with string instead (*Y1, Y2 Everyday materials*).

Figure 7.15 Camp furniture

Make something to attract the attention of passing ships

This might be a noise-maker or it could be something that requires bulbs and batteries or it may be a tall structure with a flag flying from it. Provide a large selection of resources and let the children decide (*Y4 Sound, Y3 and Y6 Light. Y1, Y2 Everyday materials*).

Plenary

Children exhibit their ideas and, if possible, structures can be tested or cans opened.

Follow-up ideas

If model structures have been made, the most successful solution to the problem could be scaled up to real size.

If the children have identified what is in the cans, they could design and cook a castaway meal using the cans and a selection of 'local' fresh vegetables.

Extension

Challenge the children to cope with unfamiliar resources. Can they join wood or cardboard without using tape and glue? Are they able to work out how to make a circuit from wire and bulbs without useful clips and holders? If they need to measure something, can they design and make their own tape measure?

Support

Provide useful extra resources that may help children to produce a successful product. For structural projects, allow access to construction kits and provide glue and wire plant ties instead of string. For electrical projects, leave the bulbs in their familiar bulb holders and provide wires with clips.

Have a hint sheet with pictures of possible solutions.

How to calculate the volume of a balloon

You will need:

scientific calculator   ruler

3 bricks or heavy books  balloon

1. Put two bricks at the 0 cm end of the ruler.

2. Lay the balloon on the ruler and push it gently against the bricks, using the third brick to hold it in place.

3. Carefully remove the balloon without disturbing the bricks. Measure the gap between the bricks. This is the DIAMETER of the balloon.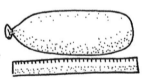

4. Divide the DIAMETER by 2 to get the RADIUS.

5. If you use a sausage-shaped balloon, you will need to measure the length as well.

6. Use a calculator to work out the volume:

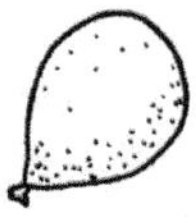

   Round balloon: $\frac{4}{3} \times (\text{RADIUS})^3 \times \pi$

   Sausage balloon: $(\text{RADIUS})^2 \times \text{length} \times \pi$

Figure 7.16

How to make a straw squeaker

You will need: paper straws
(about 10 cm long)

scissors

1. Press one end of the straw together to flatten it.

2. Cut the flattened end to a point.

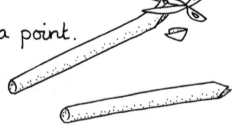

3. Put the pointed end into your mouth, just behind your teeth so that your lips meet below the cut part. The two points need to be very close together. Blow hard.

4. If the straw gets too wet, it won't squeak. Let it dry and try again.

5. Try making squeakers of different lengths.

squeak!

Figure 7.17

How to turn a needle into a compass

You will need: a needle ✎   a bar magnet 📦

a compass ❋   a dish of water and
some polystyrene

1. Hold the needle at the end with the hole in it and stroke one pole of the magnet along the needle, always in the same direction, about ten times.

Lift the magnet away from the needle to start next stroke

This way only

2. Test your needle compass: float the needle on a small piece of polystyrene in a dish of water.

The needle should settle N-S. Check it with a compass.

3. If necessary, repeat steps 1 and 2.

Figure 7.18

CHAPTER 8

Chocolate

8.1 How strong is chocolate?

8.2 Percentages

8.3 Chocolate wrappers

8.4 Flat-pack building

8.5 Making chocolate

8.6 Market research

OVERVIEW

This chapter focuses on chocolate, both as a food and as a structural material. Children investigate some of the properties of chocolate that make it a tasty food but also look at the structure of chocolate bars, using techniques used by real engineers investigating structural materials.

HEALTH AND SAFETY

Maintain strict hygiene rules at all times. The chocolate should only be consumed if you are absolutely certain that it is safe to do so. Be aware of any food allergies.

Chocolate melts satisfactorily at 50°C; care should be taken with hot water and hot melted chocolate.

Make sure tea lights are on heat-proof mats or in a tray of sand. Tie back long hair and be aware of dangling scarves and ties.

HOW STRONG IS CHOCOLATE?

Objective

- To investigate the strength of different types of chocolate bar.

Curriculum links

Mathematics

Y3: **Measurement:** measure, compare, add and subtract: lengths (m/cm/mm); mass (kg/g).
Y4: **Measurement:** find the area of a rectilinear shape by counting squares.
Y4: **Statistics:** interpret and present discrete and continuous data using appropriate graphical methods, including bar charts and time graphs.

Science

Y3: **Forces and magnets:** recognise that forces can be pushes or pulls.

Background

Structural engineers must make sure that the materials they use are strong enough for purpose. There are tests available that can be used to measure strength under various conditions and that have been standardised to allow comparison between different materials or different shapes of materials. This test measures the load-bearing strength of chocolate if it were to be used as a table top or roadway of a bridge. The chocolate bar experiences both compression and tension as it bends under the weight of the load hanging from it. If it cannot withstand the load, it will crack on the underside and collapse.

The authors are grateful to Dr Sally Organ at the Open University for her kind permission to use this activity idea.

Resources

- Finger-shaped chocolate bars
- Two bricks or wooden blocks
- Force meters – ideally push meters
- 100 g masses
- String

- Ruler
- Photocopiable: How to make a push meter (p. 131)

Introduction

Show the children the chocolate bars and ask them which one will be strongest and which they think will snap most easily. Show them what the bars look like inside.

Ask children what made them choose a particular bar. Encourage them to talk about the thickness of the bar and the structure of the inside.

Demonstrate how to test the strength and how to measure the cross-sectional area of the bar.

Main session

Children test their predictions by recording the force needed to break the bar. This could be a push force or a measure of the maximum mass the bar can support (Figure 8.7). Mass can be converted to a force in Newtons by multiplying kg by 10.

Place a folded towel under the test rig so that damage of the table is prevented if a large force is required to break the bar.

The children should also measure the dimensions of the bars and calculate the cross-sectional area. They should record the structure of the inside of the bar too.

Keep the chocolate cool if the activity is done on a warm day.

Plenary

Discuss which bar was strongest. Plot force to break against cross-sectional area on a graph and look for a correlation between area and strength. The more measurements you can get, the more accurate the results will be.

Ask the children to decide which factors make the bars strong and which ones lead to a weak bar. For confident mathematicians, calculate the force needed per cm^2 cross section (force to break ÷ cross-sectional area). Then it is possible to compare the strength of the chocolate rather than the bar.

Ask the children to think about why chocolate manufacturers might measure the strength of their chocolate bars. What implications might strength have on packaging design and transport?

Follow-up ideas

Tape several thin bars together to give a cross-sectional area similar to one of the thicker bars and test again. Does increasing the cross section have an effect on strength?

This test can also be used to investigate other materials such as biscuits, vegetables and wood.

Ask a structural engineer or architect to talk to the children about the importance of testing structural materials. There are some impressive films on-line showing what happens when it all goes wrong – the children might be interested but be aware that there is often loss of life associated with failure of structures.

Extension

Ask the children to investigate how the strength is changed if two or more bars of the same chocolate are taped together, one on top of the other and side by side.

Build a bridge using the chocolate bars to make the roadway. Children can test how strong the bridge is by placing heavy vehicles on the bridge.

Support

Tie a string round the chocolate bar and hang 100 g masses from it rather than trying to read a force meter (Figure 8.7). Set up the apparatus so that fingers cannot be inadvertently squashed by the 100 g masses.

Figure 8.7 Measuring the maximum load a chocolate bar can hold

Limit the test to chocolate bars that have approximately the same cross section, so that the children only need consider the inside structure, or choose only solid chocolate bars, with different cross sections.

PERCENTAGES

Objective

- To investigate the properties of chocolates containing different percentages of cocoa.

Curriculum links

Mathematics

Y3: Measurement: compare duration of events.
Y5: Number-fractions: recognise the per cent symbol (%) and understand that per cent relates to 'number of parts per hundred'.
Y6: Ratio and proportion: solve problems involving the calculation of percentages […] and the use of percentages for comparison.

Science

Y4: States of matter: observe that some materials change state when they are heated or cooled, and measure or research the temperature at which this happens in degrees Celsius.
Y5: Properties and changes of materials: demonstrate that […] changes of state are reversible changes.

Background

Different types of chocolate contain different percentages of cocoa. The higher the percentage the more bitter the chocolate is. Sweet milk and white chocolate contain about 30% cocoa while dark chocolate contains from 70% upward. The percentage shows how much of the chocolate, by weight, is made from cacao beans. The percentage includes the cocoa and any cocoa butter or cocoa solids added. Looking at the ingredients lists on chocolate bars will tell you that there are more differences than just cocoa percentage, but this is a good starting point for an investigation. Holding chocolate in a warm hand will cause it to melt and some types of chocolate melt faster than others. This activity measures the effect of heat on chocolate. It is difficult to measure a melting point for chocolate with any accuracy, so this activity focuses on observing the different responses to heat by the various types of chocolate.

Activity

Resources

- 30%, 70% and 85% chocolate bars
- Tea-light heating apparatus (Figure 8.8)
- Foil pie dishes
- Heat-proof mat or sand tray
- Small glass beaker, jar or bowl
- Water
- Thermometers
- Stirrers: match sticks or lolly sticks

Introduction

Show the children the chocolate bars and discuss what the percentage value means. Some will have tasted the higher percentage chocolate and know that it tastes bitter.

Show the percentages pictorially if necessary, so that the children can see the differences between the bars.

Ask whether the percentage of cocoa makes a difference to the chocolate, apart from altering the taste. Children could try snapping squares off bars of different types or holding two different types of chocolate in their hands and noting what happens.

Main session

The children investigate the melting properties of each type of chocolate. There are several ways to do this:

1   Make a water bath using a glass jar and room-temperature water (Figure 8.8). Put the chocolate into a foil container, which will float in the jar. Heat up the water using the tea light and measure the temperature of the water, which causes the chocolate to melt. The chocolate should be stirred carefully throughout. The water should not need to be much hotter than 40°C so a tea light provides a useful source of gentle heat. Using grated chocolate speeds up the process. Note that melting chocolate directly over a flame often leads to burning.

Figure 8.8 Tea-light water-bath heating apparatus – the glass jar is supported by two foil-wrapped pieces of wood

2 Melt the chocolate in a water bath of about 50°C (hot tap water) and then allow the chocolate and water to cool down. Melted chocolate does not set very obviously, so the children can drag a match stick through the melted chocolate. When the chocolate no longer flows back to fill the track of the match stick it can be considered as set. They can record which type of chocolate sets at the hottest temperature. The temperature of the water will give an approximate setting/melting point. Use only a small amount of chocolate to do this test so that the chocolate will be at the same temperature as the water.

3 Measure the time taken for each type of chocolate to melt in water at about 50°C. The chocolate that melts the fastest is likely to have the lowest melting point. The one that takes longest to melt will have the highest melting point.

If possible, the children can record the melting temperatures for each type of chocolate, also noting down the percentage of cocoa. Results could be presented as a table or a graph.

Plenary

Ask the children to say how the melting properties of the chocolate altered with changing percentage. Did the chocolate that melted the fastest also set the fastest? Did the re-set chocolate look and feel like the chocolate broken off the bar? How had it changed? Discuss fair tests and ask children which variable was changed in this test.

Ask the children to think about whether chocolate melts in their mouths and why this might make it tastier than if it remained set and hard.

Follow-up ideas

Melt the chocolate at an appropriate temperature and pour it into moulds to make chocolate figures.

Test the strength of the different chocolates by melting each one and forming it into a bar shape before testing, see 'How strong is chocolate?'.

Extension

Melt two different types of chocolate, mix them together thoroughly and allow the mixture to set. Investigate the melting properties of the 'new' chocolate. Calculate the new percentage as an average of the two percentages used.

Support

Children could investigate dark and milk chocolate. The percentage of cocoa changes depending on the manufacturer, but there is a higher percentage of cocoa in dark chocolate.

Use method 3: measure the time taken for each type of chocolate to melt in water at about 50°C.

CHOCOLATE WRAPPERS

Objective

- To use nets to produce suitable packaging for chocolates or other sweets.
- To consider what materials would make the most appropriate packaging materials.

Curriculum links

Mathematics

> **Y2: Geometry:** identify and describe the properties of 2-D shapes, identify and describe the properties of 3-D shapes.
> **Y6: Geometry:** recognise, describe and build simple 3-D shapes, including making nets.

Science

> **Y2: Uses of everyday materials:** identify and compare the suitability of a variety of everyday materials […] for particular uses.
> **Y5: Properties and changes of everyday materials:** compare and group together everyday materials on the basis of their properties including […] conductivity (electrical and thermal).

Background

Chocolates come in many attractive forms of packaging. Some will be simply folded into coloured plastic or paper while others will be packed into rectangular boxes and others into more complex-shaped cartons. The packaging materials have been chosen to protect the chocolate; many boxes have a shaped insert and soft, cushioned paper separating the layers. Paper wrappers are often lined with foil to prevent damage by damp. Thick, insulating packaging can prevent damage from heat. While plastic wrappers are effective packaging materials, they are less easily recycled. The children can consider all these things as they design their own packaging.

Activity

Resources

- Chocolate or sweets: use a bar of chocolate broken into squares
- Paper: plain copier paper, tissue paper and greaseproof paper
- Thin card
- Foil
- Nets for boxes
- Examples of chocolate wrappers and boxes
- Scissors
- Glue and tape

Introduction

Introduce the task: to wrap up some chocolates so that they are kept dry and cool and are protected from damage. The wrappings should also be attractive and eye-catching.

Show the children examples of wrappings and discuss the reasons for the various different materials.

Main session

Children investigate the materials on offer and decide which will be appropriate for packaging their chocolates. If there is time, the children could look in depth at properties, testing each material to see whether it is waterproof or light-proof.

Using nets and the examples of chocolate packaging, the children design and make their own packaging. They can decorate the packaging if there is time.

Provide the chocolate wrapped in cling film. While this is time-consuming preparation, it will avoid the problem of the chocolate melting as it is handled. It also helps maintains hygiene standards so that the chocolate could eventually be eaten.

Plenary

Children present their design ideas and show the finished product.

The packaging can be tested for various properties such as shock protection, waterproofing and lightproofing.

Follow-up ideas

The children could add the information that is found on all food packaging: nutritional details, ingredients, place of manufacture etc.

Ask a representative from a chocolate manufacturer to talk to the children about engineering suitable packaging.

Extension

Use more complex nets such as star shapes and polygons or allow children to design their own nets.

Challenge the children to make a box with a separate lid that fits over the lower part, rather than just a flap on a hinge.

Can the children wrap up a bar of chocolate in a single sheet of paper like the more expensive brands?

Support

Provide net templates for appropriate-sized boxes.

Collect the inside parts of chocolate boxes (plastic inserts, spongy paper layers), which the children can use in their own packaging.

FLAT-PACK BUILDING

Objective

- To use the properties of melted and set chocolate to produce a 3-D structure that is assembled from a 2-D template.
- To use nets to make boxes.

Curriculum links

Mathematics

Y6: Geometry: recognise, describe and build simple 3-D shapes, including making nets

Science

Y4: States of matter: observe that some materials change state when they are heated or cooled, and measure or research the temperature at which this happens in degrees Celsius.
Y5: Properties and changes of materials: demonstrate that [...] changes of state are reversible changes.

Background

Flat-pack furniture has been around for decades and flat-pack houses are now becoming popular too. Flat-packing provides all the components for a structure, ready formed and cut to the correct size and shape. With ever more sophisticated computer-aided design available, more complex structures can be designed, which can be built in a factory and then transported to site where they can be assembled quickly and efficiently. Nowadays, 3-D printers are also being used to produce more complex components for assembly. In this activity the children can design a box or small house and, using nets of 3-D shapes, can convert their designs into a 'flat-pack'. Chocolate can be melted and poured or piped into the correct shapes and, once set, can be joined together to produce a 3-D structure.

Activity

Resources

- Chocolate: either blocks to be melted or 'writing chocolate', available in tubes from cake and sugar-craft suppliers
- Piping bag and suitable nozzle, if using melted chocolate
- Ice packs
- Transparent film e.g. plastic file wallet
- Cling film
- Thin card
- Examples of nets of 3-D shapes

Introduction

Discuss the principle of flat-pack furniture and houses. How are they designed? What basic shapes are used to make a cupboard? If possible, have a small flat-packed box that can be taken apart and reassembled.

Relate the discussion to nets. Look at a cube net and ask the children to cut the net into pieces along all the fold lines. They will then be left with a 'flat-pack cube'. Can they reassemble it?

Explain that the children will use chocolate to make a flat-pack kit for a box or house. Once they have a design and have tested it using card, they can use melted chocolate to make the components and, eventually assemble their box or house. Remind them about melting and setting points for chocolate and discuss the conditions needed to make the chocolate runny or hard.

Main session

Children design their box or house using nets to help them. Once they have a design, they can make a prototype in card to check that the components all fit together as required.

Once everything is tested and accurate, the design should be transferred to clear plastic film using a permanent marker. Cover the plastic film with a layer of cling film and place this template on an ice pack to keep it cold.

Using the melted chocolate or writing chocolate, the children can draw the outlines of each component. Once these have set, the inside of each shape can be filled in and details or decoration added.

Once the chocolate is set and hard, the shapes can be peeled carefully off. Final assembly will involve more melted chocolate to be used as glue. This will be harder to cool effectively so try to keep handling to a minimum.

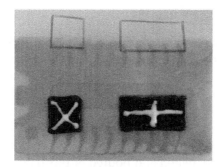

Figure 8.9 A flat-pack chocolate box under construction

Plenary

Children can discuss the success or otherwise of their designs. They should consider whether it was easier to construct the structure in card or chocolate.

A prize could be awarded for the most successful work.

Follow-up ideas

Using the writing chocolate 'pens', the children could try 3-D printing by adding a layer of chocolate at a time to build a 3-D structure. This needs very cold working conditions to be successful and is very messy.

Children could research real chocolate constructions and see how the construction methods differ to theirs. They could investigate the various ways that chocolate is shaped and piped in the confectionary industry.

Extension

Ask the children to produce a house with a pitched roof. They will need to consider the shapes for the sides of the house and consider how long the roof panels should be.

Children could make more complex 3-D shapes such as pyramids or hexagonal boxes.

Figure 8.10a The components of a house with a pitched roof

Figure 8.10b The assembled house

Support

Provide pre-cut shapes for the children to use as templates for their design.

Use sweet moulds to produce the chocolate shapes. These will produce a more accurate shape but the chocolate needs to be removed with care.

Build the boxes with ready-made thin chocolate squares or make log cabin style houses with stick-shaped chocolates.

If chocolate cannot be used, then commercial royal icing, which comes in many attractive colours, could be used instead. This will need to dry out to harden but no heat is required. Icing glue can be used to stick the units together.

MAKING CHOCOLATE

Objective

- To make chocolate from basic ingredients.

Curriculum links

Mathematics

Y2: Measurement: choose and use appropriate standard units to estimate and measure […] mass (kg/g); […] to the nearest appropriate unit, using scales.

Y5: Measurement: use all four operations to solve problems involving measure […] using decimal notation, including scaling.

Science

Y2: Living things and their habitats: describe how animals obtain their food from plants […] and name different sources of food.

Y3: Animals, including humans: identify that animals including humans need the right types […] of nutrition.

Y6: Animals, including humans: recognise the impact of diet, exercise, drugs and lifestyle on the way their bodies function.

D&T

Cooking and nutrition

KS1: understand where food comes from.

KS2: […] know where and how a variety of ingredients are grown, reared, caught and processed.

Background

Chocolate is an ancient food. In 300 BC, the Mayans grew cocoa trees and used cocoa pods as a currency. Later, the Aztecs copied the Mayans. They drank a mixture of fermented cocoa beans and spices, which they thought helped them to communicate with their gods. When the Spanish conquered Mexico in the 16th century, they sent the first cocoa beans to Europe. In the 17th and 18th centuries, drinking chocolate was very fashionable among the nobility, and confectioners created the first chocolates to eat. Chocolate was recommended as a tonic by doctors. By the 19th century, chocolate manufacture was industrialised and thousands of bars could be produced. For the first time, chocolate was available to all, not just the wealthy. Europeans eat the most chocolate, with the Swiss being the highest consumers and Great Britain not far behind. With all this chocolate being eaten, it is worthwhile knowing how to make it!

Activity

Resources

- Ingredients: cocoa powder, butter, milk, icing sugar and water
- Mixing bowls
- Spatula or large spoon for mixing
- Access to a fridge or freezer
- Access to a microwave or boiling water
- Photocopiables: Chocolate: from bean to bar (p. 130); How to make chocolate (p. 132)

Introduction

Ask the children how to make chocolate. Do they know what ingredients are in a bar of chocolate? It may surprise them to know that it can be as simple as cocoa, butter and sugar.

Explain how chocolate is made from cocoa beans (Figure 8.11). The children could be given the six pictures with the numbers deleted from Figure 8.11 and try to arrange them in the correct order.

Main session

Children make chocolate following a suitable recipe (see Resources). The recipe provided is a very simple no-cook method, although there must be some means available to melt butter, either a microwave or a boiling-water bath. The recipe produces enough chocolate for a whole class to taste. There are other simple recipes available on the internet. The chocolate produced is soft at room temperature so it is wise to store it in a fridge. As the children cook, they could taste the mixture at various points. Cocoa is very bitter; it is only when sugar is added that it becomes palatable.

The recipe produces a rich, fairly bitter chocolate. Once the children have tasted the chocolate they could plan to add dried fruit, nuts, cereal or flavourings such as mint or vanilla to their mixture.

Check allergies: soya or coconut milk can be used instead of dairy milk. Butter can be replaced with a vegan alternative such as sunflower spread. There are simple dairy-free and vegan chocolate recipes on-line.

Plenary

Children can taste their own chocolate and evaluate it. They could think about taste, texture, smell and appearance. Alternatively, arrange a taste test with each product tasted by a panel of 'judges'.

Remind children about healthy eating and having a balanced diet. Now they know what is in chocolate, they are better able to consider why it is something to eat only in small amounts! Link to the healthy eating plate used in science.

Follow-up ideas

Send the recipe home with the children and encourage them to make chocolate with a parent or carer. They could try adding flavours that reflect their culture.

Children could design chocolate bars for a particular purpose. An explorer's bar might be packed with energy-giving extras such as raisins and nuts.

Extension

Children could scale up or scale down the recipe to make a larger or smaller amount of chocolate.

The percentage figure on a chocolate bar shows how much of the bar by weight is cocoa. Children could calculate the percentage of their own chocolate. The percentage of cocoa in the chocolate from the recipe in this book is $(100 \div 280) \times 100 = 36\%$.

Support

Use measuring cups to measure the ingredients rather than weighing. Many recipes provide quantities in 'cups' as well as weights.

MARKET RESEARCH

Objective

- To design market-research questions that will provide useful data.
- To present data in a suitable visual format, such as a bar chart.

Curriculum links

Mathematics

Y2: Statistics: interpret and construct simple pictograms, tally charts, block diagrams and simple tables, ask and answer questions about totalling and comparing categorical data.

Y3: Statistics: solve one-step and two-step questions [...] using information presented in scaled bar charts, pictograms and tables.

Science

Working scientifically

KS1: gathering and recording data to help in answering questions.

Lower KS2: gathering, recording, classifying and presenting data in a variety of ways to help in answering questions.

Upper KS2: reporting and presenting findings from enquiries, including conclusions, causal relationships and explanations of and degree of trust in results.

Y1: Animals, including humans: [...] say which part of the body is associated with each sense.

D&T

Evaluate

KS1: explore and evaluate a range of existing products.

KS2: investigate and analyse a range of existing products.

Background

All designers of new products must conduct market research. There is absolutely no point in designing and producing a new product if no one wants to buy it. It may be something that will be energy-saving, money-saving or life-saving, but if members of the public are not interested, then it will not sell. Market research helps designers, and companies, to pitch their new product correctly. They may be able to highlight particular aspects of the new product, which will make it seem more desirable, once they understand what their target audience is interested in. Market research involves collecting and analysing data. This activity suggests various data-collection ideas that children could try before they draw conclusions about the likes and dislikes of their peers and other groups of children or adults.

Activity

Resources

- Squared paper
- Chocolate – amounts and types dependent on the questions to be answered

Introduction

Using a selection of chocolates, ask the children to vote on their favourite. Try to include a chocolate that children will not like (coconut-filled or bitter chocolate may be good choices). Once everyone has decided and voted, display the results as a bar chart.

Discuss why manufacturers still make the coconut or bitter chocolate when it seems that 'no one' likes it. Discuss how different people have different tastes. Children may know adults who love coconut-filled chocolates.

Explain what market research is. Some children may have experienced this as there are often market researchers in shopping centres and department stores, asking passers-by to taste a new product. Ask why it is necessary to test potential new products.

Explain that in order to make a new and popular bar of chocolate, it would be necessary to discover what members of the public like. Ask children for ideas about what questions could be asked and what data collected.

Main session

Children design and prepare their questions. They then ask a suitable 'focus group' to give their opinions or answers. Using the data collected, the children can draw bar charts or pie charts to present their data pictorially. They might start by surveying their peers but then extend the survey to a wider range of people.

Ideas for research questions:

1 *What is your favourite chocolate?* Offer a selection of suggestions. After a trial run of this question, the chocolate selection may have to be changed to include other popular varieties.
2 *Is it possible to distinguish between different brands?* Use blind tasting to discover whether there is any difference between chocolate from different manufacturers. Choose several milk chocolate bars from different chocolate manufacturers and allow the participants to taste them knowing what they are. Then ask them to try to distinguish each bar in a blind tasting. They should consider the aroma, feel of the chocolate in the mouth and taste in their analysis.
3 *Do the large tubs always contain the same numbers of each of the different chocolates?* It always seems that in a tub of mixed chocolates, there are far fewer of the chocolates one likes best. Is this true? Children can count the varieties in a tub and record how many of each

there are. They could also carry out a survey to find out which are the most popular varieties.

4 *Does everyone like the same type of chocolate?* Adults and children often have different tastes. The children can ask adults to choose their favourite chocolate, and compare the data to those collected from their peers. They should consider why there are differences, so they could also ask participants to explain their choices.

5 *How does the taste of chocolate change around the world?* The children can taste chocolate produced in different countries and try to describe the taste and texture. Many countries have their own chocolate manufacturers and it is possible to pick up examples at airports or in 'world food' sections of large supermarkets. The children can compare the percentage of cocoa in the chocolate and also look at the other ingredients. This may require some translation, but bars bought at airports or made for export often have an English ingredients list too.

6 *How many different types of chocolate are available?* This is a big question to answer. It requires research on-line and in a variety of shops. Manufacturers' websites may list the brands they sell but there are also many small, local artisan manufacturers. The results will be interesting but will time-consuming to collect.

Plenary

Children present their findings.

Collate all the results and try to decide what an ideal chocolate bar would be like. It might be a plain milk-chocolate bar or it may need to contain additions such as nuts, fruit or flavourings. The bar may be solid chocolate or a chocolate-wrapped soft centre.

Follow-up ideas

Using the details of the perfect bar, children can design a new chocolate bar. If, from their market research, the children know that this bar does not yet exist, they could send their ideas to a chocolate manufacturer. If nothing else, they should get a letter back commenting on their design and ideas. In the best case, it may well lead to an interesting collaboration with the manufacturer.

Extension

Ask children to consider sample size. Will knowing what 30 10-year olds like be a really accurate measure of the tastes of the 66 million people living in the UK? The children can consider how to make their survey more representative. They might decide to ask children and adults of different ages. They may decide to ask far more children, perhaps by making contact with other local schools or via social media.

Support

Provide pre-drawn axes so that the children can record results straight onto a bar chart.

Chocolate : from bean to bar

1. Harvest the cocoa pods.

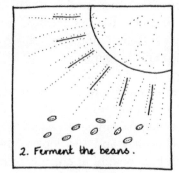

2. Ferment the beans.

3. Process the beans to remove leaves and soil.

4. Roast the beans.

5. Grind the beans to paste.

6. Mix with other ingredients.

Figure 8.11

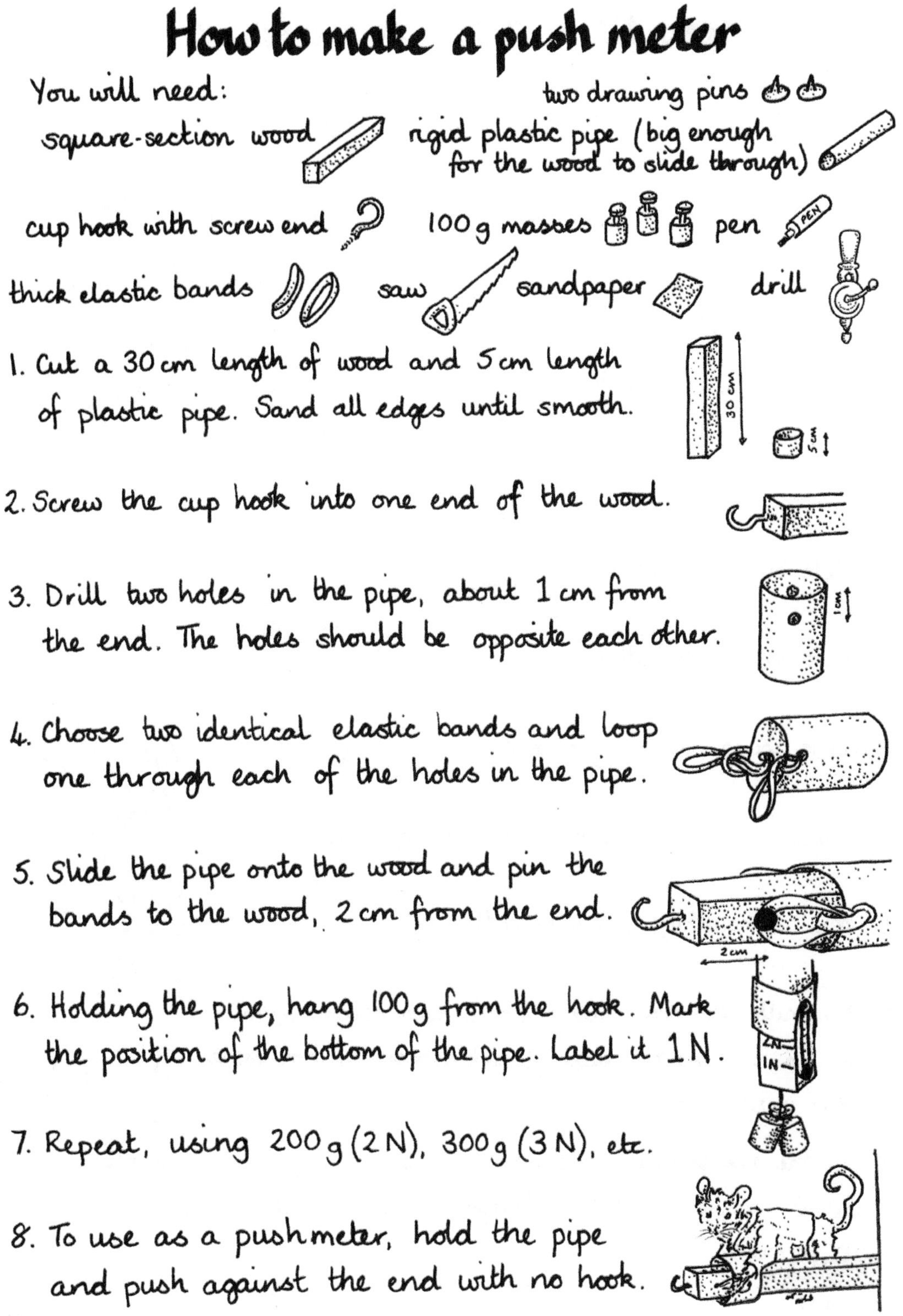

How to make a push meter

You will need: two drawing pins

square-section wood   rigid plastic pipe (big enough
                              for the wood to slide through)

cup hook with screw end   100 g masses   pen

thick elastic bands   saw   sandpaper   drill

1. Cut a 30 cm length of wood and 5 cm length
   of plastic pipe. Sand all edges until smooth.

2. Screw the cup hook into one end of the wood.

3. Drill two holes in the pipe, about 1 cm from
   the end. The holes should be opposite each other.

4. Choose two identical elastic bands and loop
   one through each of the holes in the pipe.

5. Slide the pipe onto the wood and pin the
   bands to the wood, 2 cm from the end.

6. Holding the pipe, hang 100 g from the hook. Mark
   the position of the bottom of the pipe. Label it 1 N.

7. Repeat, using 200 g (2 N), 300 g (3 N), etc.

8. To use as a push meter, hold the pipe
   and push against the end with no hook.

Figure 8.12

How to make chocolate

You will need: 100 g cocoa powder   80 g butter

100g (or more) icing sugar   2 tablespoons milk

water   sieve   bowl   tablespoon
                                       mixing spoon

microwave   greaseproof paper
or pan of hot water   rolling pin

1. Melt butter in bowl.

2. Sieve cocoa into butter.

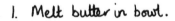

3. Sieve icing sugar into mix.

4. Taste and add more sugar if required.

5. Mix thoroughly, until smooth.

6. For milk chocolate, add 1 or 2 tablespoons of milk.
   For dark chocolate, add 1 tablespoon of hot water.
   Mix until smooth.

7. Put the mix between two sheets of greaseproof paper and roll out.
   Cut it into pieces. Chill in fridge overnight or, better still,
   in freezer.

Figure 8.13

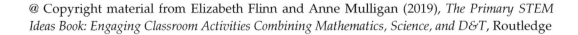

CHAPTER 9

Up, up and away

9.1 Paper planes

9.2 Jet engines

9.3 Rockets

9.4 Catapults

9.5 Parabolas

9.6 Payloads

OVERVIEW

Birds, insects and bats do it, so why can't humans fly? These activities investigate some of the principles of flight.

HEALTH AND SAFETY

Make sure planes, rockets and catapults are launched in a defined area and away from other children. Arrange a firing area into which no one should walk without warning. If working with a group, have the children standing back-to-back and firing away from each other.

Goggles should be worn when catapults and stamp rockets are being fired.

If working outside on a windy day, launch planes, rockets and catapults in the direction the wind is blowing to ensure that they fly away from the children around the launch site.

When investigating jet engines, ensure the flight-path strings are above children's head height. Warn adults in the room about the hazards.

PAPER PLANES

Objective

- To make paper planes and use fair testing to investigate the effects of changing various variables.

Curriculum links

Mathematics

Y2: Measurement: choose and use appropriate standard units to estimate and measure length/height in any direction (m/cm), mass (kg/g); […] to the nearest appropriate unit using rulers, scales.

Y6: Measurement: calculate the area of parallelograms and triangles.

Y5: Statistics: solve comparison, sum and difference problems using information presented in a line graph.

Y6: Statistics: interpret and construct […] line graphs and use these to solve problems.

Science

Y2: Uses of everyday materials: identify and compare the suitability of a variety of everyday materials […] for particular uses.

Y5: Forces: explain that unsupported objects fall towards the Earth because of the force of gravity acting between the Earth and the falling object.

Y5: Forces: identify the effects of air resistance.

Background

Gliders, flying squirrels and seeds all float effortlessly through the air. The large surface area of their wings provides sufficient air resistance to keep them airborne without the need for propellers or engines. The force of gravity acting on any airborne object will eventually cause it to fall to the ground. However, as things fall they experience air resistance, which pushes in the opposite direction. With a large-enough surface for the air resistance to act on, the effects of gravity can be counteracted somewhat, slowing the fall and, given a good push off, allow the object to travel some distance before hitting the ground. Gliders can also take advantage of thermals (hot air that is rising) to keep them aloft for longer. Specific wing shapes can also provide lift to help in sustaining flight, although this will not be covered in this activity.

Folding and flying paper planes is an enjoyable way to investigate some of the mechanics of gliding flight. Many children are able to make paper planes but it appears to be a vanishing art. This is a cheap and cheerful activity that children love and that will be remembered for long afterwards.

Activity

Resources

- A4 copier paper
- A selection of different types and sizes of paper
- Paperclips
- Photocopiables: How to make a paper plane 1 and 2 (pp. 147, 148)

Introduction

Show the children how to fold a simple paper plane. Throw the plane and watch its flight. Ask the children to describe what happens: does the plane fly up and then down or does it dive straight away; how far does it glide? If appropriate, discuss how the wings are used to maintain flight. Compare the flight of a plane and a twisted paper 'stick'. Measure and compare the distance travelled. How much of the distance travelled is due to the force of the launch and how much is due to air resistance pushing up on the wings?

Explain that there are many things that could be changed about the plane. Make a list of the children's suggestions of variables that can be changed and discuss fair testing.

Explain the task: children are going to investigate the different variables and hopefully come up with a design for a better paper plane.

Main session

Children make and test their paper planes. Two resource sheets are provided to help with making paper planes. (The plane on sheet 1 is slightly easier to make.) They record which one flies the furthest.

Testing could include the following:

- *Size*: use A5, A4 and A3 paper to make the same model of plane. Children could calculate the surface area of the wings by assuming that they are triangle-shaped.
- *Weight*: fold the same model of plane using tissue paper, printer paper, sugar paper, thin card and thicker card. The models could be weighed and their mass recorded. Graphs showing flight distance plotted against mass could be recorded to investigate whether there is a correlation between the two factors.
- *Balance*: add paper clips to the nose or fuselage of the plane to make its flight more level.
- *Model*: using the same size paper, children make various different models. This could involve an internet search where there are many useful sites giving instructions for folding good planes.

Plenary

Children present their results. Using their ideas, create the 'perfect plane'. Make it and test it. It may be better than the original or it may fail. If it fails, this is an opportunity to point out how some of the adjustments may interfere with each other to cancel out the positive effects. More work can be done, changing one thing at a time to work out what the problem may be.

Follow-up ideas

Investigate gliding in nature (See the related activity in Chapter 5: 'Defying gravity').

Design new paper plane models and provide folding instructions.

Go large! Make some enormous paper planes and try to fly them. Children could consider the limitations of paper as a material for large planes.

Figure 9.7 A paper plane made from A0 paper

Extension

Children could find their own paper-plane instructions on-line or in books and try to follow the instructions to fold the plane independently. There are some complex designs available, which produce excellent planes, but which require some thought and concentration to fold the paper correctly.

Support

Choose the simplest paper plane design and pre-fold or mark the paper ready.

Use commercial pre-printed and marked paper-plane kits.

JET ENGINES

Objective

- To demonstrate the power of air under pressure.

Curriculum links

Mathematics

Y2: Measurement: choose and use appropriate standard units to estimate and measure length/height in any direction (m/cm) […] to the nearest appropriate unit using rulers.

Y3: Measurement: measure, compare, add and subtract: lengths (m/cm/mm), compare durations of events [for example, to calculate the time taken by particular events or tasks].

Science

Y5: Forces: No direct links but extends learning and knowledge of forces.

D&T

Technical knowledge

KS1: explore and use mechanisms in their products.

KS2: understand and use mechanical systems in their products.

Background

To fly, an aircraft must have a high-speed flow of air passing over its carefully shaped wings. The aerofoil shape of an aircraft wing produces lift, which allows aircraft to get off the ground. In order to move fast enough to produce lift, the first flying machines used propellers to pull the aircraft through the air. However, in the quest for faster flight, propellers were replaced by the jet engine which pushes the aircraft through the air. The modern jet engine was designed by

Frank Whittle. Air is pulled in at the front of the engine by a fan, mixed with fuel and ignited, and the exhaust gases are ejected under pressure. Newton's third law states that for every force, there is an equal and opposite force. So, as the gases blast out backwards, the equal, opposite force pushes the aircraft forwards. This activity mimics the blast of exhaust gases using the release of air under pressure from a balloon.

Resources

- Model aircraft
- Sausage-shaped balloons
- Fishing line or thin, strong, smooth string
- Force meters or push meters
- Double-sided tape
- Two pegs
- Photocopiable: How to make a push meter (p. 149)

Introduction

Throw the model aircraft and discuss how far it flew and how fast. Ask the children to explain what made it move forwards through the air and what made it stay up and fly. Ask them how real aircraft move through the air. Some children may suggest propellers and some may suggest jet engines.

Explain how an aircraft can only stay aloft if air is moving over and past its wings. As soon as the air stops moving, the aircraft falls. Demonstrate by holding up the model aircraft and dropping it. It may fly a short distance, but not as far as when thrown. Ask how a propeller might make air move over the wings?

Tell the children about Frank Whittle's invention. Jet engines blast compressed gases out of the back of the engine. This pushes the aircraft forwards through the air. Explain that the activity will demonstrate how this works. You may have to explain that the air in a balloon is compressed by the balloon pump.

Main session

Set up one or more string 'flight paths' across the room. Aim to have them above head height for the children and keep the string as taut as possible. Hook a model aircraft onto each string (Figure 9.8). Ask the children to push or pull the model aircraft along the string with a force meter and measure the force needed to move them. If you have push meters, the children can time the aircraft's journey as they push it along the string at a constant force.

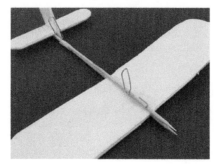

Figure 9.8 A home-made model plane with opened-out paper clips used to hang it from the string

Blow up two sausage-shaped balloons to approximately equal sizes and clip the ends closed with pegs. Using double-sided tape, attach a balloon to each wing. These represent the jet engines. Release both pegs simultaneously and watch the aircraft. It should move very rapidly along the string.

If you can find a propeller-driven model aircraft, wind up the propeller and watch how the aircraft moves along the string. Is it as fast as the 'jet'? Can the children explain why?

Plenary

Discuss the force needed to move the model aircraft and the distance it moved if pushed with a particular force. Ask the children to consider the force that the jet-engine balloon must have provided.

Ask the children to predict what would happen if the balloons were pumped up more or less. How would that affect the compression of the air and the speed of the aircraft? Can they see a link? What would happen if there were four balloons rather than two? If possible, test this.

Follow-up ideas

Children could investigate the jet engine and look on-line or in books for explanations about how it works.

Rockets are launched when the massive downwards force of compressed exhaust gases from the engines pushes them off the ground. Children could try to launch small rockets up a vertical string using balloon jets (Figure 9.9).

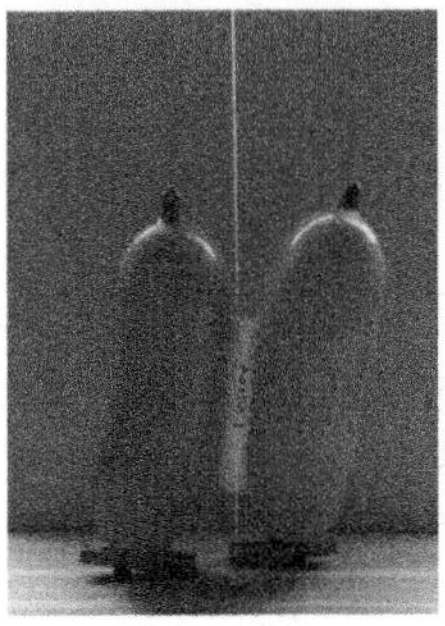

Figure 9.9 A balloon-powered rocket – with these two balloons, it travelled to the ceiling in about two seconds

Extension

The children could try measuring the speed of the jet-propelled aircraft. Mark a start and stop point on the string and use a stopwatch to time the journey. Measure the speed of an aircraft pushed along with a 1 N force and larger forces, if possible. Using a graph of force against speed, it may be possible to work out the force provided by the balloons.

Support

Show the children what happens with various sized balloons. Ask them to link balloon size to speed or distance travelled.

Hold a pumped up balloon securely so it will not fly away and release the air onto the children's hands so that they can feel the force.

ROCKETS

Objective

* To investigate simple forces.

Curriculum links

Mathematics

Y2: **Measurement:** choose and use appropriate standard units to estimate and measure length/height in any direction (m/cm), mass (kg/g); [...] to the nearest appropriate unit using rulers, scales.

Science

> **Y3: Forces and magnets:** No direct links but provides a good introduction to forces.
> **Y5: Forces:** No direct links but extends learning and knowledge of forces.

Background

Resources

- Bendy straws
- Paper cut into 10 cm × 10 cm squares
- A pencil
- Sticky tape
- Photocopiable: How to make a paper rocket (p. 150)

Introduction

Demonstrate how the paper rocket is launched (see Resources) and ask about the force provided by blowing. Is it a push or a pull and why does it move the rocket?

Show the children how to make their rockets and explain what they will be trying to find out.

Main session

Children make the rockets and investigate how they can make them fly as far as possible. This may involve blowing harder, launching the rocket at a particular angle or adjusting the rocket (perhaps by using less paper or adding a nose cone). Measure the distance travelled.

Children could decorate or name their rockets to avoid mix ups.

Figure 9.10 Paper rockets – even with a small force, these can travel up to 1 m

Plenary

Organise a competition to see whose rocket flies furthest.

Discuss the reasons why some rockets flew further than others. Emphasise how forces were involved in this flight, both to launch the rocket and to slow it down in flight

Follow-up ideas

Go large! Make large rockets that can be launched from a plastic pipe, using a plastic 2 l drink bottle to provide the pneumatic force.

Figure 9.11 A big rocket-launch system made from two plastic overflow pipes linked with a 135° joint with a bicycle inner tube used to connect the bottle the system has been glued to a plank for stability

Children can investigate how real rockets are launched. They could find out why the rocket engines fire downwards but the rocket goes up. This is a good introduction to Newton's third law: every action (force) has an equal and opposite reaction.

Extension

Investigate whether the length or mass of the rocket has an effect on the distance it can travel.
Add fins, wings or a nose cone to the rocket to see whether the flight time can be increased.

Support

Help with rolling the paper and taping will be required. However, these rockets will launch and fly successfully even if not tightly rolled!

CATAPULTS

Objective

- To investigate how making changes to a catapult influences the flight of the projectile fired from it.

Curriculum links

Mathematics

Y2: Measurement: choose and use appropriate standard units to estimate and measure length/height in any direction (m/cm), mass (kg/g); […] to the nearest appropriate unit using rulers, scales.

Science

Y3: Forces and magnets: notice that some forces need contact between two objects.
Y5: Forces: identify the effects of [forces] that act between moving surfaces.

Background

Catapults work by converting the energy stored in a stretched elastic band (strain energy) into movement (kinetic energy). The more energy that is put into stretching the elastic (the more it is stretched), the faster the projectile will move on release. The first law of thermodynamics states that energy is neither created nor destroyed, but just converted from one form to another. This activity demonstrates this. While these are small catapults, it is worthwhile remembering that larger catapults can be used to launch jets from aircraft carriers.

Resources

- A catapult
- Projectiles (dowels, lolly sticks, chopsticks, straws)
- A selection of elastic bands of different thickness, length and colour
- Targets
- Measuring tape
- Goggles
- Photocopiable: How to make a catapult (p. 151)

Introduction

Fire the catapult and ask the children to explain why the projectile moves. If appropriate, talk about the energy transferred. The energy required to stretch the elastic band comes from the food we eat and the energy in the food comes, via the food chain, from the Sun. The stretch energy is converted into movement energy as the projectile flies. Once the projectile has landed, the movement energy has been converted into heat (from friction due to air resistance) and sound energy. So, firing the catapult has actually warmed up the air!

Ask the children what might change the distance the projectile travels. Create a list of variables that could be changed.

Main session

Children investigate the catapults. Ask children to aim towards a target: a bucket or a pile of paper cups offer attractive targets, rather than just firing randomly.

Children could try stretching the elastic band by different amounts or use different thickness elastic bands or different length/mass projectiles. They should measure the distances travelled, or their success in hitting a target as they make changes.

Plenary

Children report back and try to explain what they have discovered. They should explain, if they can, how and why the forces involved have been changed by their alterations.

Follow-up ideas

Go large! Make a large catapult using scrap wood and dressmakers' elastic. Make a sturdy base that can be sat on to steady the framework when launching the projectile. Launch a ping-pong ball or tennis ball rather than a stick.

Figure 9.12 Balls launched from this large catapult flew 20 m but it took time to develop a good launching technique

Use the catapult to investigate parabolas and payloads (described later in this chapter).

Extension

Adjust the shape of the projectile to make it less streamlined. Add lumps of modelling clay or flaps of paper. Measure which projectile flies furthest. This will involve making sure the elastic is stretched the same amount each time.

Investigate the theory that a projectile fired horizontally hits the ground at the same time as an identical projectile that is simply dropped from the same height.

Support

Mark out distances clearly, using coloured paper flags, so that the children can see easily how far their projectile flew. Test fire first to see the distances covered by the projectiles (normally not more than a couple of metres at best).

Use square cross-section wooden projectiles as these are easier to hold on the catapult.

PARABOLAS

Objective

- To investigate how the length of flight of a projectile is influenced by the angle of take-off.

Curriculum links

Mathematics

Y2: **Measurement:** choose and use appropriate standard units to estimate and measure length/height in any direction (m/cm) […] to the nearest appropriate unit using rulers.
Y5: **Geometry:** know angles are measured in degrees: estimate and compare acute, obtuse and reflex angles, draw given angles, and measure them in degrees (°).
Y6: **Statistics:** interpret and construct […] line graphs and use these to solve problems.

Science

Y5: **Forces:** explain that unsupported objects fall towards the Earth because of the force of gravity […].
Y5: **Forces:** identify the effects of air resistance.

Background

A parabola is a symmetrical, n-shaped curve with some special properties. The path of any projectile under the influence of gravity follows a parabolic curve. So, watching the path of flight of a football kicked upwards, one can see that it follows a curve, first climbing as it moves forward, reaching a maximum height and then falling in a curve symmetrical to the climb curve (Figure 9.13). In terms of the speed, the ball gets slower and slower as it moves up, until it is stationary at the highest point of the path, it then accelerates as it falls again. Changing the angle of take-off changes the shape of the parabola and thus the distances travelled both vertically and horizontally. There is an optimum take-off angle for the longest flight (45°). A cannon ball follows a parabolic curve when it is fired from a cannon. In battle, flight distances could vary depending on the distance of the cannon from the target. The soldiers would use a few test shots to calculate the best angle to use to reach the enemy's stronghold.

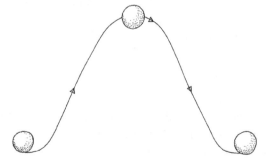

Figure 9.13 Parabolic flight

Resources

A rocket and launcher: this could be a stamp rocket, a pumped-water rocket or a paper
rocket (see Rockets activity)
A protractor
Measuring tape

Introduction

Show the children pictures of a cannon or an archer and the path of the flight of a cannon ball
or arrow. Discuss which force causes the cannon ball or arrow to fall to the ground. Look at
the pattern of flight. Ask the children to describe the shape of the flight path. The children can
think about why it is this shape and how gravity affects the flight. Ask what would happen
to the horizontal distance travelled if the angle of take-off was altered.

Main session

Using the rocket kit, fire off a few rockets at different angles. Try vertically and horizontally
and a random angle in between. Measure the distance travelled horizontally by the rocket.

The children then use their rocket and launcher to find the best angle of take-off. They
can use trial and improvement or they could use a protractor to measure the launch angle
and increase this in 10° or 5° increments. Some rockets come with adjustable launch pads. If
not, then use a stiff piece of card or wood as a ramp (Figure 9.14)

Figure 9.14 A paper rocket on a launch ramp – the ramp is taped to the table and the small block of wood
can be slid to and fro to adjust the angle

Children should consider how to ensure that this is a fair test. For example, they should
not vary the force with which they fire the rocket.

The distance travelled for each launch angle can then be plotted on a graph or shown
pictorially.

Plenary

Discuss what the best angle for the longest flight was. Look at pictures of parabolas and discuss how the launch angle and the distance travelled are linked to the maximum height of
the rocket.

Follow-up ideas

Use a catapult to fire balls or sticks at different angles. Do the same rules apply? Which angle
gives the longest distance?

Children could research Galileo's work on inertia, which helped him to explain the parabolic path of arrows.

Extension

Set the children a challenge to find the correct angle of launch to hit a target at a particular distance. They should be able to use their data to calculate this.

Support

Mark some angles on a piece of card, which can be used to change the angle of the launch pad. Projectiles fly longest if launched at 45° so make sure that is included.

PAYLOADS

Objective

- To investigate how to move heavy loads by air.

Curriculum links

Mathematics

Y2: **Measurement:** choose and use appropriate standard units to estimate and measure length/height in any direction (m/cm), mass (kg/g); […] to the nearest appropriate unit using rulers, scales.

Science

Y5: **Forces:** identify the effects of air resistance.

Background

Anyone who has flown on a commercial airline will know that there is a luggage weight limit and that on a partially empty flight passengers are sometimes redistributed around the cabin. This activity allows children to investigate what needs to be changed if a flying vehicle is to carry a heavy load. The vehicle might be a rocket taking equipment to the International Space Station, a cargo aircraft taking aid to a disaster area, or even a seed being blown away from the parent plant. In every case, the weight of the cargo is limited by the design of the vehicle and the design of the vehicle is determined by the expected load.

Resources

- Cargo: a collection of objects of the same mass and size, which can be loaded onto the flying vehicle. This might be paper clips, seeds, 1 p coins or Lego® bricks
- A flying vehicle: a foam rocket from a stamp-rocket set, a paper aircraft, a projectile for a catapult, a helium balloon etc.
- Launching equipment as required: stamp-rocket base, catapult, strong throwing arm etc.
- Glue and tape
- Measuring tape
- Weighing scales (balance)

Introduction

Decide what vehicle the children will be using. Talk about transporting cargo by air. What are the problems? What cargo might be moved and why? Ask the children what might happen if too much cargo was loaded? Ask them how they might alter the vehicle to allow it to carry more.

Main session

Starting with an unloaded vehicle, the children measure how far it can fly. They then gradually load it up with cargo. With each addition, the flight distance is measured and recorded. Note that most rockets and paper aircraft can carry more than a dozen paper clips so the children may find it less time-consuming to load cargo in batches of five or ten rather than one at a time.

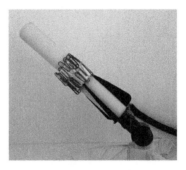

Figure 9.15 A rocket with a 30-paperclip payload ready to launch

When the vehicle can no longer leave the launch pad, or if it crashes immediately on launching, record the number of units of cargo and, if possible, weigh the load.

The children should now consider how they could alter the vehicle to allow it to continue to fly even with the cargo. This might mean making bigger or stiffer wings, launching with more force (equivalent to using more fuel) or even completely redesigning the vehicle or the launch mechanism.

The redesigned system can then be tested again.

Plenary

Discuss the results. What were the heaviest loads that could be successfully transported? What were the best alterations? Discuss why the alterations work: larger wings will provide greater air resistance and prevent the vehicle falling too fast, more force can lift the vehicle higher against gravity, so it has further to fall and will take longer to hit the ground.

If the children have been studying plants in science, this is a perfect opportunity to look at seed dispersal and consider the shapes of wind-dispersed seeds. Children could design wind-dispersed seeds rather than aircraft and rockets for this activity (see the related activity in Chapter 5: 'Defying gravity').

Follow-up ideas

This is a very rough-and-ready test. Children can consider how to ensure that it is a fair test.

Think about where the best place to put the cargo is. Consider symmetrical and non-symmetrical loadings and look at the results (see the related activity in Chapter 4: 'Cargoes').

Extension

Add in a financial factor. Carrying more cargo earns more money, but adjustments, including using more fuel, cost money. The children can decide when redesign is no longer economical. They may also be able to find a cheaper way to alter the vehicle.

Surface area of wings is a key factor in extending flight times. Children could calculate the surface areas and plot against flight distances to see whether there is a correlation.

Support

Provide two different vehicles for the children to test. One should be able to carry more cargo perhaps due to having larger wings, or being larger.

If using a stamp rocket, launch the rocket with two different forces: a gentle push using one hand, and a proper stamp. The children can load the rocket with different weight cargoes and see which launch force allows it to go further. This can be related to fuel use if appropriate.

How to make a paper plane (1)

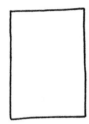  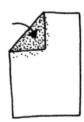

1. Choose a piece of paper.   2. Fold in half, lengthwise.   3. Open out and fold one corner in to meet centrefold.

4. Repeat with opposite corner.   5. Fold sloping edge to meet centrefold.   6. Repeat with opposite edge.

7. Fold paper in half along centrefold.   8. Fold the wings.   9. Ta da!

Figure 9.16

How to make a paper plane (2)

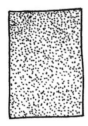  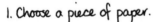 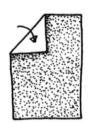

1. Choose a piece of paper.   2. Fold in half, lengthwise.   3. Open out and fold one corner in to meet centrefold.

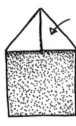  

4. Repeat with opposite corner.   5. Turn over. Fold sloping edge to meet centrefold.   6. Repeat with opposite edge.

7. Fold point down to meet the edges from 5 and 6.   8. Fold paper in half.   9. Fold the wings.

10. Ta da!

Figure 9.17

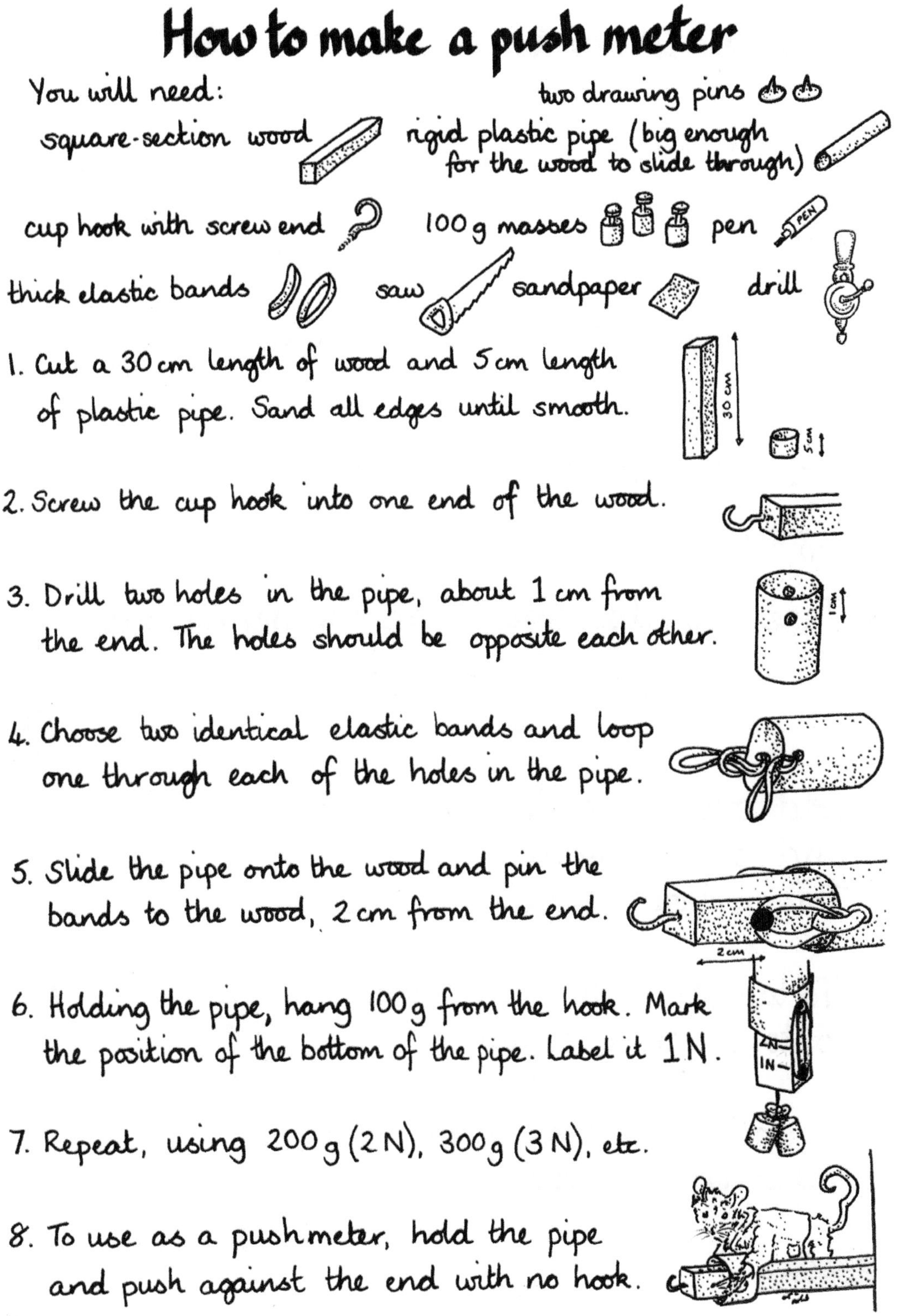

How to make a push meter

You will need:

square-section wood   two drawing pins

rigid plastic pipe (big enough for the wood to slide through)

cup hook with screw end   100g masses   pen

thick elastic bands   saw   sandpaper   drill

1. Cut a 30cm length of wood and 5cm length of plastic pipe. Sand all edges until smooth.

2. Screw the cup hook into one end of the wood.

3. Drill two holes in the pipe, about 1cm from the end. The holes should be opposite each other.

4. Choose two identical elastic bands and loop one through each of the holes in the pipe.

5. Slide the pipe onto the wood and pin the bands to the wood, 2cm from the end.

6. Holding the pipe, hang 100g from the hook. Mark the position of the bottom of the pipe. Label it 1N.

7. Repeat, using 200g (2N), 300g (3N), etc.

8. To use as a push meter, hold the pipe and push against the end with no hook.

Figure 9.18

How to make a paper rocket

You will need:

paper scissors pencil tape bendy straw

1. Cut a square of paper, 10 cm × 10 cm.

2. Roll the paper round a pencil, as tightly as you can.

3. Tape the edge and slide the pencil out.

4. Fold one end of the paper tube and tape it shut. This is your rocket!

5. To launch: push the rocket onto a bendy straw...

   ...and blow sharply through the other end of the straw.

Figure 9.19

How to make a catapult

You will need:
small piece of wood, about 15 cm wide

thick elastic bands

two drawing pins

dowel or 0.5 cm square-section wood

1. Stretch an elastic band around the wood.

2. Press drawing pins into the edges of the wood, just below the elastic band (to stop it slipping).

press → ← press

3. Pull the middle of the elastic band down, lower than the pins.

↓ pull

weeeeee!!

4. Place the dowel with one end touching the band. Grip the band and dowel between finger and thumb, as shown by the arrows.

grip → ← grip

wooosh

5. Aim and fire! Pull down until the band is stretched, then let go.

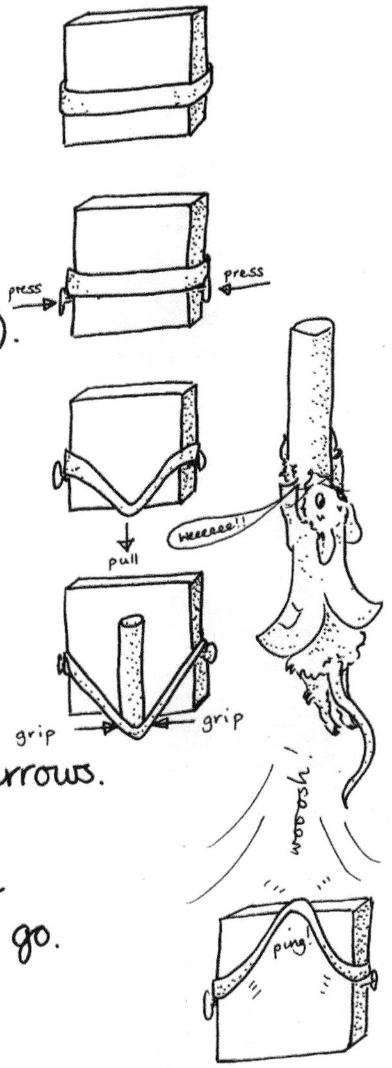

ping!

Figure 9.20

CHAPTER 10

STEM beyond the curriculum

10.1 Who forged the cheque?

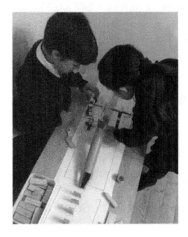

10.2 Chain reaction

10.3 Building with triangles

10.4 Sorting machines

10.5 Packing puzzles

10.6 Makey Makey

OVERVIEW

The activities in this chapter offer opportunities to use mathematics, science and D&T knowledge in an interesting and stimulating way and give children the opportunity for some problem-solving and reasoning. However, there are not always clear links to the primary curriculum for science or mathematics. While the activities could be used in lessons, they are also ideal for use as holiday projects, STEM-club activities or for special events such as a STEM Day or Science Week.

HEALTH AND SAFETY

As with all activities involving construction, care should be taken to ensure that there are safe areas to walk and defined areas for using scissors, saws and glue.

Be aware of water spills during chromatography sessions.

Makey Makey is safe and there should be no risk of electric shock, but warn children that humans are conductors and therefore they should be very careful when dealing with electricity.

WHO FORGED THE CHEQUE?

Objective

- To use paper chromatography to analyse different inks.
- To investigate the solubility of inks.

Curriculum links

Mathematics

There are no direct National Curriculum links.

Science

Y5: **Properties and changes of materials:** know that some materials will dissolve in liquid to form a solution.

Y5: **Properties and changes of materials:** use knowledge of solids, liquids and gases to decide how a mixture might be separated.

Background

Chromatography is a process used to separate mixtures. Most substances have differing properties in solvents such as water or acetone. This can be exploited by chemists who wish to analyse the mixture. As the dissolved mixture moves through or across a solid material, the components separate out, depending on how they interact with the solid. The simplest form of chromatography uses water as the solvent and the dissolved mixture is then allowed to spread out across a filter paper. The coloured pigments making up the ink move at different speeds and separate out into different coloured streaks, producing what is known as a chromatogram. Chromatography is used to analyse inks as in this activity, but also to check the components of medicines and other chemicals for impurities or unexpected forms of a chemical. An advantage of chromatography is that only very small samples are required so it is very useful in crime-scene investigations and in drug or pollution testing.

Resources

- Five or six different pens with the same coloured ink (blue or black) numbered or labelled so each can be identified. Include: felt-tip pens, biros, handwriting pens, fountain pens and gel pens. Felt-tip pens work best (see Figure 10.8)
- A selection of different coloured felt-tip pens
- Filter paper cut into small 10 cm × 2 cm strips
- Small beakers or jars
- Water
- Pencils
- A chromatogram of the ink from one of the pens – make sure it is unique and cannot be linked to more than one pen
- Photocopiable: How to investigate ink using paper chromatography (p. 168)

Introduction

Set the scene: A cheque has been forged using the head teacher's signature and someone has managed to run off with thousands of pounds from the school account! The thief must be caught. Thankfully, the school has managed to get hold of the forged cheque from the bank and the ink used to sign it has been analysed. Show the chromatogram of the ink used in the forgery. Several (fictional) people are suspected and pens have been taken from their pencil cases and desks for analysis. Once it is known which pen did the writing, the crook can be apprehended.

Main session

Introduce the concept of chromatography and let the children try it out using felt-tip pens. Avoid using the pens of the colour chosen by the forger. Show the children how the colours of each pen become separated during chromatography. Discuss what colours make up each ink.

Figure 10.7 Two children can easily share one set of apparatus

Once the children understand the concept of how to test inks for the 'hidden' colours, they can analyse the pens from the suspects. One should have the same chromatographic profile as the ink from the cheque. Allow the children access to the chromatogram of the ink from the forgery so that they can compare their results.

Plenary

Children present their evidence, identifying the thief. They should explain how they came to their conclusions.

Older children will realise that this is 'pretend' but can be easily persuaded to enjoy the activity and have fun trying to find the thief. Young children may take it all seriously and be worried by the thought of a criminal in school. Adjust the story accordingly.

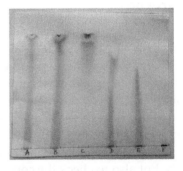

Figure 10.8 A chromatogram of six different blue pens
Note: A: fountain pen; B and C: felt-tip pens from different manufacturers; D: gel pen; E: technical drawing pen; F: biro.

Figure 10.9 Solving the crime – this is a particularly good activity for encouraging team work: the boys are holding their chromatographic evidence having solved the crime!

Follow-up ideas

Try mixing two colours of felt-tip pen ink on one chromatogram. Then ask the children to find out which two colours were mixed by testing combinations of pens.

Chromatography is used to identify substances in many different types of investigation. Children could try to find out more.

Extension

Calculate the Rf values for each different colour (see photocopiable sheet). This way, the results from different groups can be compared even if their chromatograms have run for different distances up the paper. The Rf value remains the same regardless of the size of the paper or the distance the water has moved.

Support

Choose three very different pens (one felt-tip pen, one biro and one handwriting pen) so that the results are really clear.

CHAIN REACTION

Objective

- To use knowledge of properties of materials to build a machine.
- To consider how a force can be moved from one object to another.

Curriculum links

Mathematics

There are no direct National Curriculum links.

Science

Y5: Forces: recognise that some mechanisms, including levers, pulleys and gears, allow a smaller force to have a greater effect.

D&T

Technical knowledge

KS1: build structures, exploring how they can be made stronger, stiffer and more stable.

KS1: explore and use mechanisms in their products.

KS2: apply their understanding of how to strengthen, stiffen and reinforce more complex structures.

KS2: understand and use mechanical systems in their products.

KS2: understand and use electrical systems in their products.

Background

Forces cause things to move or to change shape. The action of a force can be transmitted through a series of actions to a distant object. For example, think of a row of dominoes: the finger used to push the first one over never touches the last domino in the row, yet the push effect will reach it as each domino topples over and passes the push onto its neighbour. Chain-reaction machines use this idea to move a push force through a number of mechanisms from one end of a table to the other. The children's game 'Mousetrap' has a similar machine in the centre of the playing board. A series of events, set off by a rolling ball, leads to the mousetrap falling.

Resources

- Dominoes
- An example of a chain-reaction machine or videos (search the internet for 'Rube Goldberg machines')
- Paper and pens for designing
- Junk materials
- Toys: cars, action figures, train sets, marbles etc.
- Construction sets
- Table tops/space
- Scissors, saws, glue, tape, string, as appropriate

Introduction

Show the children a real chain-reaction machine or video of one. Explain to them how the falling over of the first domino leads to all the subsequent events and how the very last thing that happens is that another domino falls over, which can be used to start another machine in the chain. Point out that this is a very complex way of doing something quite simple (illustrated by this tape dispenser clip on-line: www.youtube.com/watch?v=w9CsUUXDIPo), but that it uses many properties of materials and various different types of force.

The children could look carefully at the machine or video and make a list of each separate component and the mechanism used to move the force on.

Main session

To start with, each machine can have just one action, for example, a toy train on a slope or a row of dominoes or a ball in a tipping cup. Join these units together and flick the first domino over. With some adjustments, things will go well.

Children could then design a more complex machine incorporating several different actions (Figure 10.10). They should be given some guidelines: the machine must be set off by a domino on the table top falling over and the last thing that their machine does will be to knock over another domino, also standing on the table top. If necessary, limit the size by defining the maximum area the machine can fill (the top of a table or a taped-off area of the floor).

You may like to provide some 'set pieces' that can be incorporated into the designs, for example: a runway for a marble made from plastic tubing, ping-pong balls fastened firmly to string, a circuit with a switch, which operates a fan.

If possible, allow the children to make the machines. This could be a task that they do at home with help from adults or it could be something that they do over a day during a STEM/Science Week. It needs time and patience and plenty of rethinking!

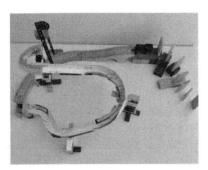

Figure 10.10 A complex but functional link in a chain-reaction machine – this machine has four different actions: a domino run; the train; a tip mechanism; and a marble run

Plenary

Carefully set up the machines and push over the first domino. How far does the chain reaction run?

Children can explain how their machine works or they can look at the next machine in the link and try to describe what will happen before it is set in motion.

Follow-up ideas

Invite other schools to join in. Ask the local secondary school to lend older pupils to help with the building and assembly.

Extension

Ask the children to include a particular element in their design (a slope, wheel, an elastic band).

Give a requirement for the machine: for example, there must be a ball that rolls down a slope or something must be lifted at least 20 cm above the table or a light bulb must be lit.

Support

Keep it simple. It may not look quite so exciting but it is more likely to work and can always be extended afterwards.

Use construction sets and toys rather than junk material for building any structures.

BUILDING WITH TRIANGLES

Objective

- To build large 3-D structures using properties of a triangle as the structural building block.

Curriculum links

Mathematics

Y1: Geometry: recognise and name common 2-D and 3-D shapes.

Y2: Geometry: identify and describe the properties of 2-D shapes, […] 3-D shapes, […] identify 2-D shapes on the surface of 3-D shapes.

Y3: Geometry: draw 2-D shapes and make 3-D shapes using modelling materials.

Y4: Geometry: compare and classify geometric shapes, including quadrilaterals and triangles, based on their properties and sizes.

Y6: Geometry: recognise, describe and build simple 3-D shapes, including making nets.

Science

Y1: Everyday materials: No direct links but extends learning.

Y2: Uses of everyday materials: No direct links but extends learning.

D&T

Technical knowledge

KS1: build structures, exploring how they can be made stronger, stiffer and more stable.

KS2: apply their understanding of how to strengthen, stiffen and reinforce more complex structures.

Background

Structural engineers and architects use different systems to create roofs that span large spaces such as airport-terminal buildings or circus tents. The problem to be solved is to provide support to the roof without it collapsing under its own weight and without filling the inside of the building with lots of supporting columns. These so-called space-frame structures are often made up from a repeated pattern of modular units. Many space-frame structures have a tetrahedron as one of the base units. Triangles are strong, stable structures and are the most rigid shapes. As a result of this strength and rigidity, triangles occur in the structures of buildings from the ancient Egyptian pyramids to modern buildings such as the Gherkin in London. In this activity, children build 3-D structures using a tetrahedron as the base shape. They also investigate how a rectangular shape can be made more rigid by using triangles.

This activity was inspired by a space-frame building activity in module T207 'Engineering: mechanics, materials, design', part of the Open University BEng course and is used here by kind permission of the School of Engineering and Innovation at the Open University (www.open.ac.uk).

Resources

- Straws, either plastic or paper: all one length or in two lengths (see Table 10.1)
- Hair grips
- Photocopiable: How to build with straws (p. 169)

Table 10.1 Cutting guide to allow reinforced squares to be assembled

Straw type	Original straw length	Shorter length for squares
Art straws (paper)	40.5 cm	28.5 cm
Drinking straws (plastic)	19.8 cm	14 cm

Introduction

Demonstrate how to make a triangular shape and then a tetrahedron using the straws and hair grips (Figure 10.11a).

If you have straws of two different lengths then show the children how to make and reinforce a cube (Figure 10.11b).

Figure 10.11a A tetrahedron

Figure 10.11b A cube made with two lengths of straw

Main session

Children build structures based on equilateral triangles and/or squares.

Once the children can build confidently with straws and hair grips, set them a challenge to build a structure. This might be a free-standing archway, a 3-D shape or a bridge.

Plenary

Ask the children about the structures. Were the triangular shapes more rigid than the square shapes? What happened if they did not reinforce the square faces with diagonals?

Follow-up ideas

The children could use this building method to try to make large versions of the various 3-D shapes they have learnt about in mathematics.

Go large! Working together, the children could try to build a structure such as an arch, big enough to crawl through.

Encourage the children to look up when they in airports or other large covered spaces. Can they spot the triangles in the roof structure?

Extension

Can the children build shapes with more than four faces? Are they rigid and stable enough for structural purposes?

Support

Join the hair clips together in twos to make building the triangular shape easier.

The children make the triangular shapes, which can then be connected to make tetrahedrons and other shapes with the help of an adult.

SORTING MACHINES

Objective

• To make a machine that can separate a mixture of items with different properties.

Curriculum links

Mathematics

There are no direct National Curriculum links.

Science

Y1: Everyday materials: compare and group together a variety of everyday materials on the basis of their simple physical properties.

Y3: Forces and magnets: compare and group together a variety of everyday materials on the basis of whether they are attracted to a magnet, and identify some magnetic materials.

Y5: Properties and changes of materials: compare and group together everyday materials on the basis of their properties including hardness, solubility, transparency, conductivity and response to magnets.

Y5: Properties and changes of materials: use knowledge of solids, liquids and gases to decide how mixtures might be separated including through filtering, sieving and evaporating.

Y5: Forces: recognise that some mechanisms, including levers, pulleys and gears, allow a smaller force to have a greater effect.

D&T

Technical knowledge

KS1: explore and use mechanisms in their products.

KS2: understand and use mechanical systems in their products.

Background

Machines are commonly used to sort mixtures of objects. In general, mixtures can be separated because non-identical objects usually have different properties. Mixtures of coins can be sorted and counted by a machine that separates the coins based on size, shape or material. Mixed recycling can be separated by a machine using the different densities of plastics and glass. Steel and aluminium cans are separated by a machine using a magnet. Once children have learnt about some of the properties of common materials, they are in an ideal position to consider how to separate a mixture. The simplest machines divide the mixture into two using one property. For example, materials that float can be easily separated from those that sink by dropping the whole mixture into a tank of water. More complex machines may be able to further sub-divide the materials by using a second property, so that the two sets of materials could then be passed over a magnet. The combinations are endless. Using a property such as size or shape means that a mixture can be more finely sorted. A series of sieves with different sized holes is used by gardeners to grade soil from fine particles to stones.

Resources

Introduction

- Mixtures: flour and paper clips, rice and pasta, match sticks and nails
- Simple separating apparatus: sieves, magnets, a bowl of water

Main session

- Mixtures: various different coins, different size beads, mixed recycling
- Junk materials including paper cups, plastic pots and cardboard
- Magnets or self-adhesive magnetic strips
- Scissors
- Glue and tape

Introduction

Prepare some mixtures. Discuss the properties of the materials in each mixture and ask the children to suggest ways to separate the mixtures. There is often more than one way to do this.

Once the children have decided on a method, test their ideas. Sometimes ideas that are good 'on paper' can be problematic in practice and it is useful for the children to see this.

Introduce some more complex mixtures. These might be: a collection of different coins; a mixture of different sized beads; a box of mixed recycling containing paper, plastic and cans. To start with, a mixture of two or three different things will be sufficient. Ask the children to suggest ways to sort the mixtures. This time, they can start to think about making their own apparatus and not be constrained by the simple apparatus on offer previously.

Main session

Working in groups, the children design their own separating machines. They should list the properties of the items in the mixture and think about how the mixture could be sorted. The children could try to sort the mixtures manually, using Venn diagrams or other sorting methods.

If possible, allow some testing to take place.

Once a suitable design has been agreed, the children can make their machine. They should use junk materials where possible rather than ready-made apparatus.

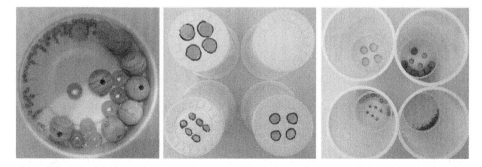

Figure 10.12 A size-sorting machine – the pots are stacked up, the mixture poured in the top and the whole thing shaken vigorously for a few minutes

Plenary

The machines can be tested using a suitable mixture. The machines can be assessed on their accuracy as well as the time taken to sort the mixture. Children can explain how they used the properties of the materials in the mixtures to help them decide how best to try to separate them.

Follow-up ideas

Sorting machines can make life easier. The children could design a machine to help people: perhaps a Lego®-brick sorter or a coin sorter to use after the summer fair when all the money needs to be counted.

Visit a garden-waste composting site or recycling depot and look at the sorting machines they use there.

Extension

Challenge the children to separate a mixture of more than three different items. Choose materials with less obvious properties.

Sorting by size usually involves several sieves through which the mixture is shaken (Figure 10.12). Ask the children to design a machine to sort by size that does not require shaking. They should consider how to move the mixture past the various sized holes, perhaps using a conveyor belt or ramps.

Support

Provide some pre-punched pots with holes of different sizes for size-sorting machines.

Start with a mixture of only two components with obvious differences.

PACKING PUZZLES

Objective

- To make a puzzle with pieces that can be arranged in various different combinations.

Curriculum links

Mathematics

Y2: **Geometry:** order and arrange combinations of mathematical objects in patterns and sequences, use mathematical vocabulary to describe position, direction and movement.

Science

Working scientifically: No direct links but encourages a search for patterns and solutions.

D&T

A good opportunity to carry out the whole Design Cycle: Research, Design, Make and Evaluate.

Background

Many of the brain-training and mind puzzle games popular these days have packing puzzles. The player is presented with a set of different sized and shaped pieces that must be fitted into a particular outline. There are often thousands of possible combinations, but it may be hard to find even one!

Puzzles like this are easy to make and manipulating the pieces until they all fit within the defined area can be very satisfying.

Resources

- Squared paper: use the largest squares available or photocopy and enlarge
- Thin card
- Laminating resources
- Pens, pencils and rulers
- Scissors
- Envelopes
- A pre-prepared, simple puzzle (see Figure 10.13)

Optional

- Balsa wood (thin sheets)
- Sandpaper
- Wood glue
- Paint suitable for wood
- Varnish
- Craft knives and cutting mats or scissors

Introduction

Show the children a pre-prepared packing puzzle. Explain the task and let the children attempt to solve the problem. They should record their solution on squared paper. The puzzle could be available for the children to try over the course of several days. Encourage the children to look for alternative solutions.

Once the children understand the concept, explain how to make a simple puzzle using squared paper:

1 Define the area of the puzzle first by drawing a clear outline.
2 Divide the area into different shaped pieces, made up of different numbers of squares.
3 Colour each piece in a different colour.
4 Cut out the shapes very carefully.
5 Try to reassemble the shapes to fit inside the original outline.

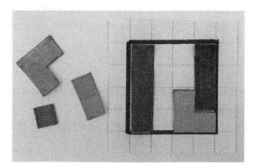

Figure 10.13 A simple packing puzzle

Main session

Using squared paper, the children design and cut out their own puzzles. It is helpful if they make a copy of their design before cutting out; this will provide a 'cheat sheet' in case the puzzle proves impossible to solve!

Encourage use of rulers for drawing the shapes neatly and accurately. The puzzles are more interesting if all the shapes are different so challenge children to go for variety.

Once cut out, coloured and tested, the puzzle can be copied onto thin card and laminated to protect the pieces.

Use an envelope to keep the puzzle pieces safe. On the outside of the envelope stick or draw the correct sized outline. This means the envelope can act as the puzzle assembly board.

The puzzles are more resilient and easier to manipulate if made from wood. Balsa wood can be easily cut with scissors or craft knives and once painted and varnished will withstand heavy use.

Plenary

Children try to reassemble their own puzzles. They can consider whether there is more than one possible solution and draw any alternative answers.

The children should evaluate the design, commenting on how neatly the pieces fit together. The more accurate the cutting, the better the puzzle will be.

Follow-up ideas

Make puzzles with a theme. Once children understand how to make these puzzles, then they can be designed to be more attractive. For example, the pieces could represent the clothes to be packed into a suitcase (Figure 10.14), or animals to be packed into a zoo.

Figure 10.14 A suitcase packing puzzle inspired by a brain-training game – the puzzle pieces have been cut from balsa wood; the pictures were designed and drawn on squared paper, which has been stuck onto the wood

Make a set of puzzles of increasing difficulty and invite older or younger children to play with them. Evaluate the success of the designs.

Choose the best puzzles to make in wood. Make a wooden tray to hold the pieces.

Extension

Encourage use of oblong outlines. This gives scope for a larger range of shapes and sizes.

Use isometric paper so that the children can create more interesting shapes using triangles. This activity could be extended to include tangrams.

Figure 10.15 A puzzle designed using isometric paper

Support

Keep the outline small, start with a 4 × 4 square.
    Enlarge the paper so that the squares are much larger.

MAKEY MAKEY

Objective

- To use suitable conductors in a Makey Makey invention.

Curriculum links

Mathematics

There are no direct National Curriculum links.

Science

Y4: Electricity: recognise some common conductors and insulators.
Y6: Electricity: No direct links but extends learning and knowledge of circuits.

D&T

Technical knowledge

KS2: apply their understanding of computing to program, monitor and control their
    products.

Background

Makey Makey is an invention kit that allows children to turn everyday items into computer
keys. Instead of pressing the space bar on the computer keyboard to advance the cursor,
the user can touch a banana or a lump of home-made play dough and the cursor will move.
With a long enough USB cable to connect Makey Makey to the computer, the 'keys' can be
situated a long way from the keyboard, so that a child in one room could control a computer in another. The 'keys' can be made out of anything that conducts electricity including
fruit and vegetables, home-made play dough and humans. Programs can be written using

coding software such as Scratch. At its most basic, Makey Makey is a simple circuit and joining the two connectors together will complete the circuit to 'press' the key on the computer. While this can be seen as a gimmick, there is a serious side to Makey Makey; it can be used to create accessible keyboards for children and adults who cannot use a conventional one. Using Makey Makey, the computer keys to play a game can be controlled by moving the head, using very small and limited finger movements or even by rolling a wheelchair to and fro.

Resources

- Makey Makey kit: one is sufficient for the whole class to share, but more would be better
- Foil
- Home-made play dough or similar, or celery or bananas to act as the 'keys'
- Card and paper
- Scissors
- Tape

Introduction

Introduce children to Makey Makey. There are videos on-line that show what sort of things can be made and there are many useful lesson plans and examples on the website: www.makeymakey.com.

Main session

Once the children are familiar with how Makey Makey works and once they understand some simple coding, they can design and make all sorts of gadgets.

Start with the coding. Using a programme such as Scratch, the children can program the computer to respond when the space key is pressed. Makey Makey can then be connected and tested. Once the children understand how to wire up the connections, they can write more complex programs requiring more keys.

Ideas for useful gadgets might include a wildlife camera trap, a door bell with video, a burglar alarm or a game that can be controlled by head movements rather than by pressing keys.

Plenary

Children can connect up Makey Makey to their computer and test their program.

Follow-up ideas

Once the children understand how everything works, they will have many follow-up ideas of their own to try out. There are plenty of games that could be invented!

The standard Y4 Electricity 'Is it a conductor?' tests could be livened up by using Makey Makey. Potential conductors could be tested using a Makey Makey unit linked to an exciting, colourful Scratch program. The children could design a program to use in another class or with a younger year group (Figure 10.16).

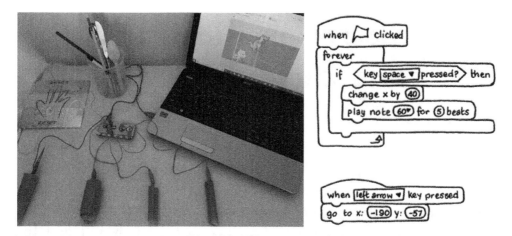

Figure 10.16 A Scratch program for testing materials to find insulators and conductors – the test material is laid across two sensors (in this case, either the two carrots or the two stalks of celery); if it conducts electricity, the character will move forward; the 'reset' button (left arrow) returns the characters to the start

Extension

Ask the children to draw diagrams to show the circuit involved. There is no circuit symbol for Makey Makey, so perhaps they could design one.

Support

There are some pre-written programs available that the children could use as a starting point before adjusting things to suit them.

Use foil rather than fruit to make the 'keys' so that the children understand they must use a conductor.

Scratch is developed by the Lifelong Kindergarten Group at the MIT Media Lab. See http://scratch.mit.edu.

Makey Makey was developed by Jay Silver and Eric Rosenbaum and is a JoyLabz product. See www.makeymakey.com.

How to investigate ink using paper chromatography

You will need: filter paper □ ⌐₁₀cm pencil ✏ felt pens ✶

water ◌ ◌ small glass jar or beaker 🥛

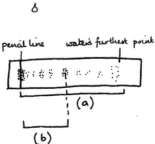

1. Cut strips of filter paper, 10 cm × 2 cm.
2. Draw a pencil line about 1 cm from one end.
3. Draw a thick felt-tip mark over the pencil line.

4. Put a small amount of water in the beaker. Carefully, lower the filter paper into the water, being careful not to get the pencil line wet.

keep pencil line above water

5. Hold the paper still and wait. The water and ink will start to move up the paper.

water's furthest point

pencil line

about 2 cm

6. When the water is about 2 cm from the top of the paper strip, remove the strip from the beaker and let it dry.

pencil line   water's furthest point

(a)

(b)

7. To find Rf value:
   - measure from the pencil line to the highest point the water reached (a).
   - measure from the pencil line to the middle of one of the coloured sections (b).
   - calculate (b) ÷ (a)

Figure 10.17

How to build with straws

You will need:

straws 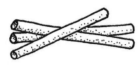   hair grips

1. Push a hair grip onto the end of a straw. One leg of the grip should be inside, one outside.

2. Link a second grip to the first.

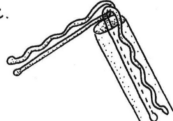

3. Push the second grip into a new straw.

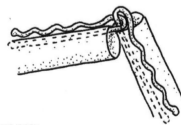

4. You can link three, four or more hair grips together to make 3D structures.

Figure 10.18